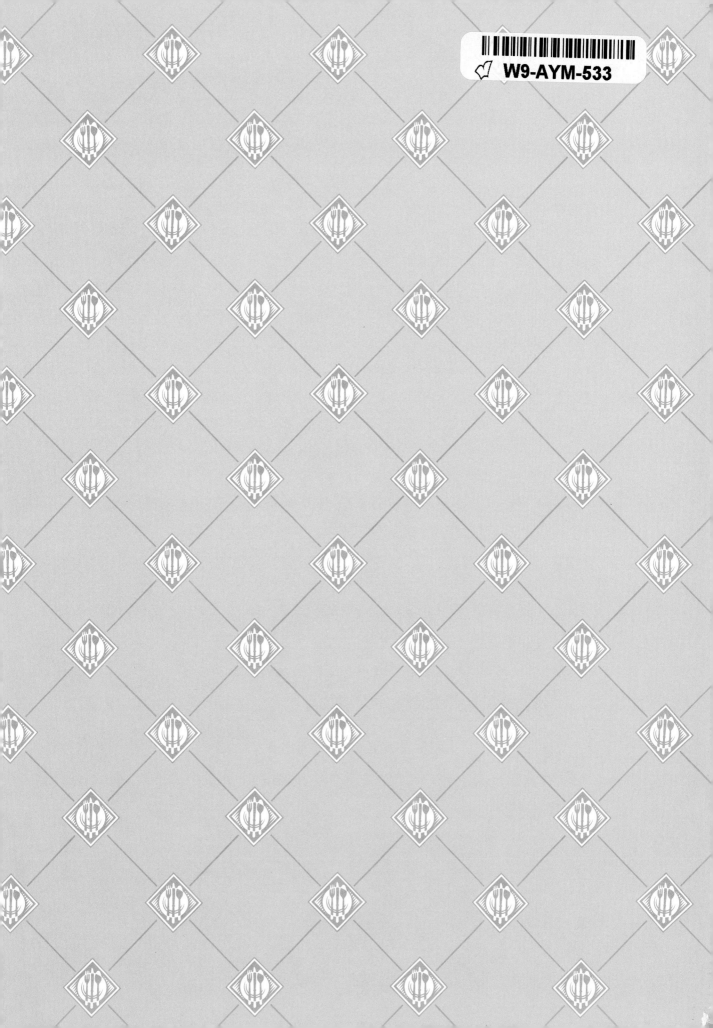

FAVORITE ALL TIME RECIPES™

PUBLICATIONS INTERNATIONAL, LTD.

Pictured on front and back covers: Almond Double Chip Cookies (page
23); Auntie Van's Christmas Cookies (page 48); Black Russian Brownies
(page 61); Cherry Pinwheel Slices (page 91); Chocolate Chips Thumbprint
Cookies (page 20); Chunky Butter Christmas Cookies (page 43); Holiday
Almond Wreaths (page 13); Linzer Tarts (page 9); Norwegian Molasses
Cookies (page 53); Peanut Butter and Chocolate Cookie Sandwich Cookies
(page 38); Pecan Turtle Bars (page 60); Raspberry Meringue Bars (page 72);
Richest Spritz (page 15); Snow Caps (page 78); Snow-Covered Almond
Crescents (page 14).

MICROWAVE COOKING
Microwave ovens vary in wattage. The cooking times given in this publication are approximate. Use the cooking times as guidelines and check for
doneness before adding more time.

Homemade
HOLIDAY COOKIES

Homespun Holiday Favorites   *4*

Chips 'n' Chocolate   *20*

From the Cookie Jar   *40*

Outrageous Brownies & Bars   *58*

Fanciful Cookies   *76*

Acknowledgments   *93*

Index   *94*

Homespun Holiday Favorites

Baking a batch of these delightful cookies will fill your home with holiday cheer.

GLAZED SUGAR COOKIES

COOKIES

1 package DUNCAN HINES®
Golden Sugar Cookie Mix

1 egg

GLAZE

1 cup sifted confectioners
sugar
1 to 2 tablespoons water or
milk
½ teaspoon vanilla extract

Food coloring (optional)
Red and green sugar
crystals, nonpareils or
cinnamon candies

1. Preheat oven to 375°F.

2. **For cookies,** combine cookie mix, contents of buttery flavor packet from Mix and egg in large bowl. Stir until thoroughly blended. Roll dough to ⅛-inch thickness on lightly floured surface. Cut dough into desired shapes using floured cookie cutters. Place cookies 2 inches apart on ungreased baking sheets. Bake at 375°F for 5 to 6 minutes or until edges are light golden brown. Cool 1 minute on baking sheets. Remove to cooling racks. Cool completely.

3. **For glaze,** combine confectioners sugar, water and vanilla extract in small bowl. Beat until smooth. Tint glaze with food coloring, if desired. Brush glaze on each cookie with clean pastry brush. Sprinkle cookies with sugar crystals, nonpareils or cinnamon candies before glaze sets. Allow glaze to set before storing between layers of waxed paper in airtight container. *Makes 2½ to 3 dozen cookies*

Glazed Sugar Cookies

SUGAR COOKIE WREATHS

1 package DUNCAN HINES® Golden Sugar Cookie Mix	Green food coloring Candied or maraschino
1 egg	cherry pieces

1. Preheat oven to 375°F. Combine cookie mix, contents of buttery flavor packet from Mix and egg in large bowl. Stir until thoroughly blended.

2. Tint dough with green food coloring. Stir until desired color. Form into balls the size of miniature marshmallows. For each wreath, arrange 9 or 10 balls with sides touching into a ring, 2 inches apart, on ungreased baking sheets. Flatten slightly with fingers. Place small piece of candied cherry on each ball.

3. Bake at 375°F for 5 to 7 minutes or until set but not browned. Cool 1 minute on baking sheets. Remove to cooling racks. Cool completely. Store in airtight container. *Makes 2 dozen cookies*

STAINED GLASS COOKIES

½ cup BLUE BONNET® Margarine, softened	1 teaspoon DAVIS® Baking Powder
½ cup sugar	½ teaspoon baking soda
½ cup honey	½ teaspoon salt
1 egg	5 rolls LIFE SAVERS® Fancy
1 teaspoon vanilla extract	Fruits Candy
3 cups all-purpose flour	

In large bowl with electric mixer at medium speed, beat margarine, sugar, honey, egg and vanilla extract until thoroughly blended. Blend in flour, baking powder, baking soda and salt. Cover; chill at least 2 hours.

On lightly floured surface, roll out dough to ¼-inch thickness. Cut dough with cookie cutters into desired shapes. Trace smaller version of cookie shape on dough leaving a ½- to ¾-inch border of dough. Cut out and remove dough from center of cookies. Place cookie outlines on baking sheets lined with foil.

Crush each color of candy separately between two layers of waxed paper with mallet. Spoon crushed candy inside centers of cookies.

Bake at 350°F for 6 to 8 minutes or until candy is melted and cookie is lightly browned. Cool cookies completely before removing from foil.
Makes 3½ dozen cookies

Sugar Cookie Wreaths

MERRY SPRITZ COOKIES

1 foil-wrapped bar
   (2 ounces) NESTLÉ®
   Premier White®
   baking bar
¾ cup (1½ sticks) butter or
   margarine, softened
½ cup sugar
½ teaspoon salt

1 egg
2 teaspoons vanilla extract
2½ cups all-purpose flour
One 9-ounce package (1½ cups)
   NESTLÉ® Toll House®
   semi-sweet chocolate
   Rainbow™ Morsels

Preheat oven to 350°F. In small saucepan over low heat, melt Nestlé Premier White baking bar; set aside.

In large mixer bowl, beat butter, sugar and salt until creamy. Blend in egg and vanilla extract. Blend in melted baking bar. Gradually beat in flour. Place dough in cookie press fitted with desired plate. Press dough onto ungreased cookie sheets; decorate with Nestlé Toll House semi-sweet chocolate Rainbow Morsels.

Bake 7 to 9 minutes until set. Let stand 1 minute. Remove from cookie sheets; cool completely. *Makes about 6 dozen cookies*

CHOCOLATE-RASPBERRY SPRITZ

1½ foil-wrapped bars
   (3 ounces) NESTLÉ®
   unsweetened chocolate
   baking bars
¾ cup (1½ sticks) butter or
   margarine, softened
1 cup sugar
½ teaspoon salt

1 egg
½ cup raspberry preserves
1 teaspoon vanilla extract
3 cups all-purpose flour
One 9-ounce package (1½ cups)
   NESTLÉ® Toll House®
   semi-sweet chocolate
   Rainbow™ Morsels

Preheat oven to 350°F. In small saucepan over low heat, melt Nestlé unsweetened chocolate baking bars; set aside.

In large mixer bowl, beat butter, sugar and salt until creamy. Blend in egg, preserves and vanilla extract. Blend in melted chocolate. Gradually beat in flour. Place dough in cookie press fitted with desired plate. Press dough onto ungreased cookie sheets; decorate with Nestlé Toll House semi-sweet chocolate Rainbow Morsels.

Bake 8 to 10 minutes until set. Let stand 1 minute. Remove from cookie sheets; cool completely. *Makes 8 dozen cookies*

LINZER TARTS

1 cup BLUE BONNET®
  Margarine, softened
1 cup granulated sugar
2 cups all-purpose flour
1 cup PLANTERS® Slivered
  Almonds, chopped

1 teaspoon grated lemon
  peel
1/4 teaspoon ground
  cinnamon
1/3 cup raspberry preserves
  Confectioner's sugar

In large bowl with electric mixer at high speed, beat margarine and granulated sugar until light and fluffy. Stir in flour, almonds, lemon peel and cinnamon until blended. Cover; chill 2 hours.

Divide dough in half. On floured surface, roll out one half of dough to 1/8-inch thickness. Using 2 1/2-inch round cookie cutter, cut circles from dough. Reroll scraps to make additional rounds. Cut out 1/2-inch circles from centers of half the rounds. Repeat with remaining dough. Place on ungreased baking sheets. Bake at 325°F for 12 to 15 minutes or until lightly browned. Remove from sheets; cool on wire racks. Spread preserves on top of whole cookies. Top with cut-out cookies to make sandwiches. Dust with confectioner's sugar.   *Makes 2 dozen cookies*

YULETIDE GINGER COOKIES

3/4 cup firmly packed brown
  sugar
1/2 cup light corn syrup
1/2 cup (1 stick) margarine,
  softened
2 egg whites, slightly beaten
3 cups QUAKER® Oat Bran
  Hot Cereal, uncooked

3/4 cup all-purpose flour
2 teaspoons ground ginger
1 teaspoon baking soda
1 teaspoon ground
  cinnamon
1/4 cup red or green colored
  sugar crystals

Heat oven to 350°F. Beat brown sugar, corn syrup and margarine in large bowl until fluffy. Blend in egg whites. Gradually add combined oat bran, flour, ginger, baking soda and cinnamon; mix well. Shape into 1-inch balls; roll in colored sugar crystals to coat. Place 2 inches apart on ungreased cookie sheet. Gently press balls into 2-inch circles. Bake 11 to 13 minutes or until light golden brown. Cool 2 minutes on cookie sheet; remove to wire rack. Cool completely. Store tightly covered.

Makes about 3 1/2 dozen cookies

Milk Chocolate Florentine Cookies

MILK CHOCOLATE FLORENTINE COOKIES

²/₃ cup butter or margarine
2 cups quick oats, uncooked
1 cup sugar
²/₃ cup all-purpose flour
¼ cup corn syrup
¼ cup milk

1 teaspoon vanilla extract
¼ teaspoon salt
One 11½-ounce package
   (2 cups) NESTLÉ® Toll
   House® milk chocolate
   morsels

Preheat oven to 375°F.

Melt butter in medium saucepan over low heat. Remove from heat. Stir in oats, sugar, flour, corn syrup, milk, vanilla extract and salt; mix well. Drop by measuring teaspoonfuls, about 3 inches apart, onto foil-lined cookie sheets. Spread thin with rubber spatula.

Bake 5 to 7 minutes. Cool on cookie sheets. Peel foil away from cookies.

Melt Nestlé Toll House milk chocolate morsels over hot (not boiling) water; stir until smooth. Spread chocolate on flat side of half the cookies. Top with remaining cookies.   *Makes 3½ dozen sandwich cookies*

SUGAR COOKIE ORNAMENTS

1 package DUNCAN HINES®
  Golden Sugar Cookie Mix
1 egg
1 teaspoon milk
  Assorted colored sugar
  crystals, cinnamon
  gems, nonpareils or
  decors

DUNCAN HINES® Vanilla
Layer Cake Frosting
(optional)

1. Preheat oven to 375°F.

2. Combine cookie mix, contents of buttery flavor packet from Mix, egg and milk in large bowl. Stir until thoroughly blended. Form dough into 1-inch balls. Place 3 inches apart on ungreased baking sheets. Grease and flour bottom of drinking glass. Press gently to flatten cookies to form 2-inch circles.

3. Press end of drinking straw into top of each cookie to make hole. Decorate cookies as desired or leave plain to frost.

4. Bake at 375°F for 5 to 7 minutes or until set but not browned. Press straw through holes in top of cookies again. Cool 1 minute on baking sheets. Remove to cooling racks. Cool completely. Frost plain cookies, if desired.

5. String ribbon through holes in cookies. Tie at top.

Makes 3½ to 4 dozen cookies

Tip: Frosting can be divided and tinted with a few drops of red and green food coloring. Stir until well blended. Frost patterns on ornaments or frost and sprinkle with decors.

Painted Ornaments: Combine 1 egg yolk and 1 teaspoon water. Stir well. Divide into 3 custard cups. Tint each with 1 drop of different food coloring. Sketch design on unbaked cookie with tip of knife. Use clean watercolor paint brushes to paint designs on cookies before baking. Bake and cool as directed.

PREMIER WHITE® SUGAR COOKIES

Two 6-ounce packages (6 foil-
    wrapped bars) NESTLÉ®
    Premier White® baking
    bars, divided
2¼ cups all-purpose flour
  1 teaspoon baking powder
¼ teaspoon salt
½ cup (1 stick) butter or
    margarine, softened

⅓ cup sugar
1 egg
1 teaspoon vanilla extract
One 9-ounce package (1½ cups)
    NESTLÉ® Toll House®
    semi-sweet chocolate
    Rainbow™ Morsels

Preheat oven to 350°F. In small saucepan over low heat, melt 3 foil-wrapped bars (6 ounces) Nestlé Premier White baking bars; set aside. In small bowl, combine flour, baking powder and salt; set aside.

In large mixer bowl, beat butter and sugar until creamy. Blend in egg and vanilla extract. Beat in melted baking bars. Gradually beat in flour mixture until soft dough forms. Shape dough into ball; flatten to ¾-inch thickness. Wrap in plastic wrap; refrigerate 15 minutes until firm.

On lightly floured surface, roll out dough to ⅛-inch thickness. With 2½- to 3-inch cookie cutters, cut dough into shapes. Place on ungreased cookie sheets.

Bake 8 to 10 minutes until edges are golden brown. Let stand 2 minutes. Remove from cookie sheets; cool completely.

In small saucepan over low heat, melt remaining 3 foil-wrapped bars (6 ounces) baking bars. Spread or pipe melted baking bars on cookies. Decorate with Nestlé Toll House semi-sweet chocolate Rainbow Morsels, attaching with melted baking bars.   *Makes about 3½ dozen cookies*

Christmas Tree Hanging Cookies: With skewer, make ½-inch hole near top edge of each cut out before baking.

HOLIDAY ALMOND WREATHS

¾ cup FLEISCHMANN'S®
   Margarine, softened
½ cup sugar
¼ cup EGG BEATERS®
   Cholesterol-Free 99%
   Real Egg Product, thawed

1 teaspoon almond extract
2 cups all-purpose flour
½ cup ground PLANTERS®
   Almonds
   Green and red candied
   cherries (optional)

In medium bowl with electric mixer at medium speed, beat margarine and sugar until light and fluffy. Add egg product and almond extract; beat well. Stir in flour and ground almonds. Using pastry bag with ½-inch star tip, pipe dough into 1½-inch wreaths, 2 inches apart, on ungreased baking sheets. Decorate wreaths with green and red candied cherries, if desired. Bake at 400°F for 10 to 12 minutes or until golden brown. Cool on wire racks. *Makes 3 dozen cookies*

SUGAR COOKIES

1 cup BUTTER FLAVOR
   CRISCO®
1 cup sugar
1 egg
1½ teaspoons vanilla

2 cups all-purpose flour
1 teaspoon baking soda
1 teaspoon cream of tartar
½ teaspoon salt

1. Cream Butter Flavor Crisco and sugar in large bowl at medium speed of electric mixer. Beat in egg and vanilla.

2. Combine flour with baking soda, cream of tartar and salt. Blend into creamed mixture. Cover and chill at least 2 hours.

3. Preheat oven to 375°F.

4. Roll out dough on floured surface to ⅛-inch thickness. Cut into desired shapes with cookie cutters. Place on ungreased baking sheets.

5. Bake at 375°F for 6 to 7 minutes. Cool on baking sheets about 1 minute. Remove to cooling racks. *Makes 5½ to 6 dozen cookies*

Note: For holidays, cut dough into desired holiday shapes. Sprinkle with colored sugar crystals before baking.

SPICED BANANA COOKIE WREATHS

2 extra-ripe, medium DOLE®
  Bananas, peeled
2 cups granola
1½ cups all-purpose flour
1 cup brown sugar, packed
1 teaspoon baking powder
1 teaspoon ground
  cinnamon
½ teaspoon ground nutmeg
¼ teaspoon salt
1 egg

½ cup margarine, melted
¼ cup vegetable oil
1 cup DOLE® Raisins
⅓ cup chopped DOLE®
  Almonds
½ cup powdered sugar
1 tablespoon milk
Candied cherries or
  colored sugar crystals
  (optional)

• Place bananas in blender. Process until puréed; use 1 cup for recipe.

• Combine granola, flour, brown sugar, baking powder, cinnamon, nutmeg and salt in large bowl. Beat in 1 cup banana, egg, margarine and oil. Stir in raisins. For each of 3 wreaths, arrange about 16 generous teaspoonfuls dough with sides touching into a ring on greased cookie sheets. Sprinkle with almonds.

• Bake in 375°F oven 15 to 18 minutes until lightly browned. Cool on baking sheets.

• Combine powdered sugar and milk in small bowl until smooth. Drizzle over cooled wreaths. Decorate with candied cherries if desired. Tie with a bow to give as a gift.   *Makes 3 wreaths (16 cookies per wreath)*

SNOW-COVERED ALMOND CRESCENTS

1 cup (2 sticks) margarine or
  butter, softened
¾ cup powdered sugar
½ teaspoon almond extract
  or 2 teaspoons vanilla
  extract
2 cups all-purpose flour

¼ teaspoon salt (optional)
1 cup QUAKER® Oats (quick
  or old fashioned,
  uncooked)
½ cup finely chopped
  almonds
Additional powdered sugar

Heat oven to 325°F. Beat margarine, powdered sugar and almond extract until fluffy. Add flour and salt; mix until well blended. Stir in oats and almonds. Using level measuring tablespoonfuls, shape dough into crescents. Bake on ungreased cookie sheet 14 to 17 minutes or until bottoms are light golden brown. Remove to wire rack. Sift additional powdered sugar generously over warm cookies. Cool completely.

Makes about 4 dozen cookies

RICHEST SPRITZ

1¼ cups confectioners' sugar
1 cup butter, softened
2 egg yolks *or* 1 whole egg
1 teaspoon vanilla extract

½ teaspoon almond extract
   (optional)
2½ cups all-purpose flour
½ teaspoon salt
   Food color (optional)

Preheat oven to 400°F. Cream confectioners' sugar and butter in large bowl with electric mixer at medium speed. Beat in egg yolks, vanilla and almond extracts. Combine flour and salt. Add to butter mixture; mix well. Tint dough with food color, if desired. Place dough in cookie press fitted with plate. Load press with dough. Press onto ungreased cookie sheets, about 2 inches apart. Decorate as desired. Bake 6 to 8 minutes or until very slightly browned around edges. Remove to wire racks to cool.

Makes about 6½ dozen cookies

Spiced Banana Cookie Wreath

ANISE PILLOWS
PFEFFERNEUSSE

1²/₃ cups all-purpose flour
1¹/₂ teaspoons DAVIS® Baking
    Powder
¹/₂ teaspoon grated lemon
    peel
¹/₄ teaspoon salt
¹/₄ teaspoon ground
    cinnamon
¹/₄ teaspoon ground nutmeg
¹/₈ teaspoon ground cloves

¹/₈ teaspoon white pepper
¹/₃ cup BLUE BONNET®
    Margarine, softened
¹/₂ cup sugar
1 egg
¹/₂ cup milk
¹/₂ cup PLANTERS® Walnuts,
    finely chopped
¹/₂ teaspoon anise seed
    Confectioner's sugar

In small bowl, combine flour, baking powder, lemon peel, salt, spices and pepper; set aside. In large bowl, beat together margarine and sugar until creamy; beat in egg. Add flour mixture alternately with milk, beating well after each addition. Stir in walnuts and anise seed. Drop dough by teaspoonfuls, 2 inches apart, on lightly greased baking sheets.

Bake at 350°F for 15 to 17 minutes. Cool slightly on wire racks. Roll in confectioner's sugar while still warm; cool completely.

Makes 5 dozen cookies

OATMEAL-BANANA LEBKUCHEN

³/₄ cup margarine, softened
¹/₂ cup brown sugar, packed
¹/₄ cup honey
1¹/₂ teaspoons ground
    cinnamon
1¹/₂ teaspoons ground ginger
1 teaspoon ground
    cardamom
¹/₂ teaspoon ground cloves
2 extra-ripe, medium DOLE®
    Bananas, peeled

2 eggs, beaten
1³/₄ cups all-purpose flour
¹/₂ teaspoon baking powder
¹/₂ teaspoon baking soda
¹/₂ teaspoon salt
³/₄ cup DOLE® Chopped
    Almonds
¹/₂ cup mixed candied fruit,
    finely chopped
2 cups quick oats, uncooked

LEMON GLAZE
³/₄ cup sifted powdered sugar
    Juice from 1 DOLE® Lemon
    (1 tablespoon)

1 drop almond extract

Continued

- Beat margarine, brown sugar and honey in large bowl. Beat in cinnamon, ginger, cardamom and cloves.

- Mash bananas with fork in small bowl; use 1 cup for recipe. Add 1 cup banana and eggs to margarine mixture; beat until blended.

- Combine flour, baking powder, baking soda and salt in small bowl. Stir in almonds and candied fruit. Add to margarine mixture. Stir until well blended. Stir in oats.

- Drop by heaping teaspoonfuls, 2 inches apart, onto greased cookie sheets. Bake in 400°F oven 8 minutes. Cool completely on wire racks. Spread with Lemon Glaze or dust with powdered sugar. When glaze has set, store cookies in airtight container.   *Makes 4 dozen cookies*

Lemon Glaze: Combine all ingredients until blended.

CHRISTMAS TREASURE NUGGETS

1 cup (2 sticks) margarine or butter, softened	½ teaspoon baking powder
1 cup firmly packed brown sugar	½ teaspoon salt (optional)
¾ cup granulated sugar	2 cups QUAKER® Oats (quick or old fashioned, uncooked)
2 eggs	2 cups QUAKER® 100% Natural Cereal, any flavor
1 teaspoon vanilla	
1¾ cups all-purpose flour	
1 teaspoon baking soda	Whole blanched almonds

Heat oven to 375°F. Beat margarine and sugars in large bowl until fluffy. Blend in eggs and vanilla. Combine flour, baking soda, baking powder and salt; add to margarine mixture and mix well. Stir in oats and cereal.

Drop by rounded teaspoonfuls, 2 inches apart, onto ungreased cookie sheet. Press 1 almond onto each cookie. Bake 8 to 10 minutes or until golden brown. Cool 2 minutes on cookie sheet; remove to wire rack. Cool completely. Store tightly covered.   *Makes 6 dozen cookies*

PEANUT BUTTER REINDEER

COOKIES
- 1 package DUNCAN HINES®
  Peanut Butter
  Cookie Mix
- 1 egg
- 2 teaspoons all-purpose
  flour

ASSORTED DECORATIONS
- Miniature semi-sweet
  chocolate chips
- Vanilla milk chips
- Candy-coated semi-sweet
  chocolate chips
- Colored sprinkles

1. **For cookies,** combine cookie mix, contents of peanut butter packet from Mix and egg in large bowl. Stir until thoroughly blended. Form dough into ball. Place flour in jumbo (15×13-inch) resealable plastic bag. Place ball of dough in bag. Shake to coat with flour. Place dough in center of bag (do not seal). Roll dough with rolling pin out to edges of bag. Slide bag onto baking sheet. Chill in refrigerator at least 1 hour.

2. Preheat oven to 375°F. Use scissors to cut bag down center and across ends. Turn plastic back to uncover dough. Dip reindeer cookie cutter in flour. Cut dough with reindeer cookie cutter. Dip cookie cutter in flour after each cut. Transfer cut-out cookies to ungreased baking sheets using floured pancake turner. Decorate each reindeer as desired. Bake at 375°F for 5 to 7 minutes or until set but not browned. Cool 2 minutes on baking sheets. Remove to cooling racks. Cool completely. Store between layers of waxed paper in airtight container. *Makes about 2 dozen cookies*

Tip: Reroll dough by folding plastic back over dough.

SANTA'S THUMBPRINTS

- 1 cup (2 sticks) margarine,
  softened
- ½ cup firmly packed brown
  sugar
- 1 whole egg or egg white
- 1 teaspoon vanilla
- 1½ cups QUAKER® Oats (quick
  or old fashioned,
  uncooked)
- 1½ cups all-purpose flour
- 1 cup finely chopped nuts
- ⅓ cup jelly or preserves

Heat oven to 350°F. Beat margarine and sugar in large bowl until fluffy. Blend in egg and vanilla. Add combined oats and flour; mix well. Shape into 1-inch balls; roll in chopped nuts. Place 2 inches apart on ungreased cookie sheet. Make indentation in center of each ball with thumb. Fill each thumbprint with about ¼ teaspoon jelly. Bake 12 to 15 minutes or until light golden brown. Cool completely on wire rack. Store loosely covered. *Makes about 3 dozen cookies*

Peanut Butter Reindeer

Chips 'n' Chocolate

Chocolate in every flavor and form is evident in this chapter—white, dark and milk chocolate in chips, glazes, fillings and more!

CHOCOLATE CHIPS THUMBPRINT COOKIES

1 cup HERSHEY'S Semi-Sweet
   Chocolate Chips, divided
¼ cup butter or margarine,
   softened
¼ cup shortening
½ cup sugar

1 egg, separated
½ teaspoon vanilla extract
1 cup all-purpose flour
¼ teaspoon salt
1 cup finely chopped nuts

Heat oven to 350°F. In small microwave-safe bowl, place ¼ cup chocolate chips. Microwave at HIGH (100%) 20 to 30 seconds or just until chocolate is melted and smooth when stirred; set aside to cool slightly. In large mixer bowl, combine butter, shortening, sugar, reserved melted chocolate, egg yolk and vanilla; blend well. Stir in flour and salt.
Roll dough into 1-inch balls. With fork, slightly beat egg white. Dip each ball into egg white; roll in chopped nuts. Place balls on ungreased cookie sheet, about 1 inch apart. Press center of each ball with thumb to make indentation. Bake 10 to 12 minutes or until set. Remove from oven; immediately place several of remaining ¾ cup chocolate chips in center of each cookie. Carefully remove from cookie sheet to wire rack. After several minutes, swirl melted chocolate in each thumbprint. Cool completely. *Makes about 2½ dozen cookies*

Chocolate Chips Thumbprint Cookies

White Chocolate Biggies and Peanut Butter Jumbos

WHITE CHOCOLATE BIGGIES

1½ cups butter or margarine,
  softened
1 cup granulated sugar
¾ cup packed light brown
  sugar
2 teaspoons vanilla
2 eggs
2½ cups all-purpose flour

⅔ cup unsweetened cocoa
1 teaspoon baking soda
½ teaspoon salt
1 package (10 ounces) large,
  white chocolate chips
¾ cup pecan halves, coarsely
  chopped
½ cup golden raisins

Preheat oven to 350°F. Lightly grease cookie sheets or line with
parchment paper. Beat butter, sugars, vanilla and eggs in large bowl until
light and fluffy. Combine flour, cocoa, baking soda and salt in medium
bowl; blend into creamed mixture until smooth. Stir in white chocolate
chips, pecans and raisins. Scoop out about ⅓ cup dough for each cookie.
Place on prepared cookie sheets, about 4 inches apart. Flatten each
cookie slightly. Bake 12 to 14 minutes or until firm in center. Cool 5
minutes on cookie sheets; remove to wire racks to cool completely.

Makes about 2 dozen large cookies

PEANUT BUTTER JUMBOS

1½ cups peanut butter
½ cup butter or margarine,
  softened
1 cup packed brown sugar
1 cup granulated sugar
3 eggs
2 tablespoons baking soda

1 teaspoon vanilla
4½ cups rolled oats, uncooked
1 cup (6 ounces) semisweet
  chocolate chips
1 cup candy-coated
  chocolate pieces

Preheat oven to 350°F. Lightly grease cookie sheets or line with parchment paper. Beat peanut butter, butter, sugars and eggs in large bowl until light and fluffy. Blend in baking soda, vanilla and oats until well mixed. Stir in chocolate chips and candy pieces. Scoop out about ⅓ cup dough for each cookie. Place on prepared cookie sheets, about 4 inches apart. Flatten each cookie slightly. Bake 15 to 20 minutes or until firm in center. Remove to wire racks to cool completely.

Makes about 1½ dozen large cookies

ALMOND DOUBLE CHIP COOKIES

¾ cup butter or margarine,
  softened
¾ cup packed light brown
  sugar
1 egg
½ teaspoon almond extract
1½ cups all-purpose flour
¼ teaspoon baking soda

Dash salt
1 cup (6 ounces) semisweet
  chocolate chips
1 cup (6 ounces) vanilla
  milk chips
½ cup slivered blanched
  almonds

Preheat oven to 375°F. Line cookie sheets with parchment paper or leave ungreased. Beat butter and brown sugar in large bowl until creamy. Beat in egg and almond extract. Combine flour, baking soda and salt in small bowl. Blend into butter mixture. Stir in semisweet and vanilla milk chips and almonds. Drop dough by rounded tablespoonfuls, 3 inches apart, onto prepared cookie sheets. Bake 8 to 10 minutes or until light brown. *Do not overbake.* Cool 2 minutes on cookie sheets; remove to wire racks to cool completely.

Makes about 3 dozen cookies

ORIGINAL TOLL HOUSE® CHOCOLATE CHIP COOKIES

2¼ cups all-purpose flour	2 eggs
1 teaspoon baking soda	1 teaspoon vanilla extract
1 teaspoon salt	One 12-ounce package (2 cups)
1 cup (2 sticks) butter, softened	NESTLÉ® Toll House® semi-sweet chocolate
¾ cup granulated sugar	morsels
¾ cup firmly packed brown sugar	1 cup nuts, chopped

Preheat oven to 375°F. In small bowl, combine flour, baking soda and salt; set aside.

In large mixer bowl, beat butter, granulated sugar and brown sugar until creamy. Add eggs, 1 at a time, beating well after each addition. Blend in vanilla extract. Gradually beat in flour mixture. Stir in Nestlé Toll House semi-sweet chocolate morsels and nuts. Drop by rounded measuring tablespoonfuls onto ungreased cookie sheets.

Bake 9 to 11 minutes until edges are golden brown. Let stand 2 minutes. Remove from cookie sheets; cool completely.

Makes about 5 dozen cookies

Toll House Pan Cookies: Preheat oven to 375°F. Prepare dough as directed; spread in greased 15½ × 10½-inch baking pan. Bake 20 to 25 minutes until golden brown. Cool completely. Cut into 2-inch squares. Makes about 3 dozen cookies.

Refrigerator Toll House Cookies: Prepare dough as directed. Divide dough in half; wrap halves separately in waxed paper. Refrigerate 1 hour or until firm. On waxed paper, shape each dough half into 15-inch log; wrap in waxed paper. Refrigerate 30 minutes.*

Preheat oven to 375°F. Cut each log into 30 (½-inch) slices. Place on ungreased cookie sheets. Bake 8 to 10 minutes until edges are golden brown. Makes 5 dozen cookies.

*Dough may be stored up to 1 week in refrigerator or up to 8 weeks in freezer, if foil- or freezer-wrapped.

Original Toll House® Chocolate Chip Cookies

Over hot (not boiling) water, melt Nestlé Toll House semi-sweet chocolate morsels, stirring until smooth; set aside.

In large mixer bowl, beat butter, sugar and vanilla extract until creamy. Beat in eggs. Stir in melted morsels. Gradually beat in flour. Cover dough; refrigerate 30 to 45 minutes.

Preheat oven to 400°F. Place dough in cookie press fitted with star plate. Press dough into 2-inch circles on ungreased cookie sheets; decorate with cinnamon candies.

Bake 5 minutes or just until set. Let stand on cookie sheets 2 minutes. Remove from cookie sheets; cool completely.

Makes about 7½ dozen cookies

CHOCOLATE MINT SNOW-TOP COOKIES

1½ cups all-purpose flour
1½ teaspoons baking powder
¼ teaspoon salt
One 10-ounce package (1½ cups) NESTLÉ® Toll House® mint flavored semi-sweet chocolate morsels, divided

6 tablespoons (¾ stick) butter, softened
1 cup granulated sugar
1½ teaspoons vanilla extract
2 eggs
Confectioners' sugar

In small bowl, combine flour, baking powder and salt; set aside. Over hot (not boiling) water, melt 1 cup Nestlé Toll House mint flavored semi-sweet chocolate morsels, stirring until smooth; set aside.

In large mixer bowl, beat butter and granulated sugar until creamy. Add melted mint flavored semi-sweet chocolate morsels and vanilla extract. Beat in eggs. Gradually beat in flour mixture. Stir in remaining ½ cup mint flavored semi-sweet chocolate morsels. Wrap dough in plastic wrap and freeze until firm, about 20 minutes.

Preheat oven to 350°F. Shape dough into 1-inch balls; coat with confectioners' sugar. Place on ungreased cookie sheets.

Bake 10 to 12 minutes until tops appear cracked. Let stand on cookie sheets 5 minutes. Remove from cookie sheets; cool completely.

Makes about 3 dozen cookies

CHOCOLATE SUGAR COOKIES

3 squares BAKER'S®
    Unsweetened Chocolate
1 cup (2 sticks) margarine or
    butter
1 cup sugar
1 egg

1 teaspoon vanilla
2 cups all-purpose flour
1 teaspoon baking soda
¼ teaspoon salt
    Additional sugar

Microwave chocolate and margarine in large microwavable bowl on HIGH 2 minutes or until margarine is melted. Stir until chocolate is completely melted.

Stir 1 cup sugar into melted chocolate mixture until well blended. Stir in egg and vanilla until completely blended. Mix in flour, baking soda and salt. Refrigerate 30 minutes.

Heat oven to 375°F. Shape dough into 1-inch balls; roll in additional sugar. Place, 2 inches apart, on ungreased cookie sheets. (If flatter, crisper cookies are desired, flatten balls with bottom of drinking glass.)

Bake 8 to 10 minutes or until set. Remove from cookie sheets to cool on wire racks. *Makes about 3½ dozen cookies*

Prep time: 15 minutes
Chill time: 30 minutes
Baking time: 8 to 10 minutes

Jam-Filled Chocolate Sugar Cookies: Prepare Chocolate Sugar Cookie dough as directed. Roll in finely chopped nuts in place of sugar. Make indentation in each ball; fill center with your favorite jam. Bake as directed.

Chocolate-Caramel Sugar Cookies: Prepare Chocolate Sugar Cookie dough as directed. Roll in finely chopped nuts in place of sugar. Make indentation in each ball; bake as directed. Microwave 1 package (14 ounces) KRAFT Caramels with 2 tablespoons milk in microwavable bowl on HIGH 3 minutes or until melted, stirring after 2 minutes. Fill centers of cookies with caramel mixture. Drizzle with melted BAKER'S Semi-Sweet Chocolate.

Top to bottom: Chocolate Sugar Cookies; Jam-Filled Chocolate Sugar Cookies; Chocolate-Caramel Sugar Cookies

CHOCOLATE MELTING MOMENTS

1 cup butter or margarine, softened
⅓ cup confectioners sugar
¼ cup unsweetened cocoa

1½ cups cake flour
Mocha Filling (recipe follows)

Preheat oven to 350°F. Lightly grease cookie sheets or line with parchment paper. Beat 1 cup butter, confectioners sugar and cocoa in large bowl until fluffy. Blend in cake flour until smooth. Shape dough into marble-size balls. (If dough is too soft to handle, cover and refrigerate until firm.) Place 2 inches apart on prepared cookie sheets. Press center of each ball with knuckle of finger to make indentation. Bake 10 to 12 minutes or until set. Remove to wire racks. Prepare Mocha Filling. While cookies are still warm, spoon about ½ teaspoonful filling into center of each. *Makes about 5 dozen cookies*

MOCHA FILLING

1 tablespoon butter or margarine
1 square (1 ounce) unsweetened chocolate

1 cup confectioners sugar
1 teaspoon vanilla
1 to 2 tablespoons hot coffee or water

Melt 1 tablespoon butter and chocolate in small heavy saucepan over low heat; stir until melted. Blend in confectioners sugar, vanilla and enough coffee to make a smooth filling.

ALL-AMERICAN CHOCOLATE CHIP COOKIES

⅔ cup butter or margarine, softened
⅓ cup shortening
1 cup packed brown sugar
½ cup granulated sugar
1 egg
1 teaspoon vanilla

2 cups all-purpose flour
1 teaspoon baking soda
1 teaspoon salt
1 package (12 ounces) semisweet chocolate chips
1 cup chopped walnuts

In large bowl, cream butter, shortening and sugars. Beat in egg and vanilla. Combine flour, baking soda and salt; stir into butter mixture, mixing well. Stir in chocolate chips and nuts. Drop by teaspoonfuls, 2 inches apart, onto greased baking sheets. Bake in 350°F oven 8 to 10 minutes, just until edges are golden (centers will still be soft). Remove to wire racks to cool. *Makes about 3 dozen cookies*

Favorite recipe from Walnut Marketing Board

CHOCOLATE MINT SUGAR COOKIE DROPS

2½ cups all-purpose flour
1¼ teaspoons baking powder
¾ teaspoon salt
1 cup granulated sugar
¾ cup vegetable oil
2 eggs
1 teaspoon vanilla extract

One 10-ounce package
    (1½ cups) NESTLÉ® Toll
    House® mint flavored
    semi-sweet chocolate
    morsels
Assorted colored sugars or
    additional granulated
    sugar

Preheat oven to 350°F. In small bowl, combine flour, baking powder and salt; set aside.

In large mixer bowl, combine granulated sugar and oil. Add eggs, 1 at a time, beating well after each addition. Blend in vanilla extract. Gradually beat in flour mixture. Stir in Nestlé Toll House mint flavored semi-sweet chocolate morsels. Shape rounded measuring teaspoonfuls of dough into balls; roll in colored sugar. Place on ungreased cookie sheets.

Bake 8 to 10 minutes until set. Let stand on cookie sheets 2 minutes. Remove from cookie sheets; cool completely.

Makes about 5½ dozen cookies

Chocolate Mint Sugar Cookie Drops

CHOCOLATE LACE CORNUCOPIAS

½ cup firmly packed brown
  sugar
½ cup corn syrup
¼ cup (½ stick) margarine or
  butter
 4 squares BAKER'S® Semi-
  Sweet Chocolate

1 cup all-purpose flour
1 cup finely chopped nuts
  Whipped cream or COOL
  WHIP® Whipped
  Topping, thawed

Heat oven to 350°F. Microwave sugar, corn syrup and margarine in large microwavable bowl on HIGH 2 minutes or until boiling. Stir in chocolate until completely melted. Gradually stir in flour and nuts until well blended. Drop by level tablespoonfuls, 4 inches apart, onto foil-lined cookie sheets.

Bake 10 minutes. Lift foil and cookies onto wire racks. Cool 3 to 4 minutes or until cookies can be easily peeled off foil. Remove foil; finish cooling cookies on wire racks that have been covered with paper towels.

Place several cookies, lacy side down, on foil-lined cookie sheet. Heat at 350°F for 2 to 3 minutes or until slightly softened. Remove from foil, 1 at a time, and roll, lacy side out, to form cones. Cool completely. Just before serving, fill with whipped cream.   *Makes about 30 cornucopias*

Prep time: 20 minutes
Baking time: 12 to 13 minutes

Saucepan preparation: Mix sugar, corn syrup and margarine in 2-quart saucepan. Bring to boil over medium heat, stirring constantly. Remove from heat; stir in chocolate until completely melted. Continue as directed.

Chocolate Lace Cornucopias

Peanut Butter and Chocolate Cookie Sandwich Cookies

PEANUT BUTTER AND CHOCOLATE COOKIE SANDWICH COOKIES

½ cup REESE'S Peanut Butter Chips

3 tablespoons plus ½ cup butter or margarine, softened and divided

1¼ cups sugar, divided

¼ cup light corn syrup

1 egg

1 teaspoon vanilla extract

2 cups plus 2 tablespoons all-purpose flour, divided

2 teaspoons baking soda

¼ teaspoon salt

½ cup HERSHEY'S Cocoa

5 tablespoons butter or margarine, melted

Additional sugar

About 2 dozen large marshmallows

Continued

CHUNKY BUTTER CHRISTMAS COOKIES

1¼ cups butter, softened
1 cup packed brown sugar
½ cup dairy sour cream
1 egg
2 teaspoons vanilla
1½ cups all-purpose flour
1 teaspoon baking soda
1 teaspoon salt

1½ cups old fashioned or
    quick oats, uncooked
1 package (10 ounces)
    vanilla milk chips
1 cup flaked coconut
1 jar (3½ ounces)
    macadamia nuts,
    coarsely chopped

Beat butter and brown sugar in large bowl until light and fluffy. Blend in sour cream, egg and vanilla. Combine flour, baking soda and salt. Add to butter mixture; mix well. Stir in oats, vanilla milk chips, coconut and nuts. Drop rounded teaspoonfuls of dough, 2 inches apart, onto ungreased cookie sheet.

Bake at 375°F for 10 to 12 minutes or until edges are lightly browned. Cool on cookie sheet 1 minute. Remove to cooling rack; cool completely.

Makes 5 dozen cookies

Favorite recipe from Wisconsin Milk Marketing Board

ORANGE SUGAR COOKIES

2 cups all-purpose flour
1½ teaspoons baking soda
½ cup FLEISCHMANN'S®
    Margarine, softened
1 cup sugar

2 teaspoons grated orange
    peel
1 teaspoon vanilla extract
¼ cup EGG BEATERS® 99%
    Real Egg Product
Additional sugar (optional)

In small bowl, combine flour and baking soda; set aside.

In medium bowl with electric mixer at medium speed, beat margarine, 1 cup sugar, orange peel and vanilla until creamy. Add egg product; beat until smooth. Gradually stir in flour mixture until blended. Cover; chill dough 1 hour.

Shape dough into 42 (¾-inch) balls; roll in additional sugar if desired. Place on lightly greased baking sheets, about 2 inches apart. Bake at 375°F for 8 to 10 minutes or until light golden brown. Remove from sheets; cool on wire racks.

Makes 3½ dozen cookies

MERRY SUGAR COOKIES

2¾ cups all-purpose flour
1 teaspoon baking soda
½ teaspoon baking powder
¼ teaspoon salt
1 cup (2 sticks) butter or
   margarine, softened
1½ cups sugar

1 egg
1 teaspoon vanilla extract
One 9-ounce package
   (1½ cups) NESTLÉ® Toll
   House® semi-sweet
   chocolate Rainbow™
   Morsels, divided

Preheat oven to 375°F. In small bowl, combine flour, baking soda, baking powder and salt; set aside.

In large mixer bowl, beat butter and sugar until creamy. Blend in egg and vanilla extract. Gradually beat in flour mixture. (Batter will be stiff.) Stir in 1 cup Nestlé Toll House semi-sweet chocolate Rainbow Morsels. Shape rounded teaspoonfuls dough into balls; place on ungreased cookie sheets. Gently press 3 or 4 remaining Rainbow Morsels into each ball.

Bake 8 to 10 minutes until edges are lightly browned. Let stand 2 minutes. Remove from cookie sheets; cool.

Makes about 4½ dozen cookies

SNICKERDOODLES

1 cup BUTTER FLAVOR
   CRISCO®
1¾ cups sugar, divided
2 eggs
1 teaspoon vanilla

2¼ cups all-purpose flour
2 teaspoons cream of tartar
1 teaspoon baking soda
¾ teaspoon salt
1 teaspoon cinnamon

1. Preheat oven to 400°F.

2. Cream Butter Flavor Crisco, 1½ cups sugar, eggs and vanilla thoroughly in large bowl at medium speed of electric mixer. Combine flour, cream of tartar, baking soda and salt. Stir into creamed mixture.

3. Shape into 1-inch balls. Combine remaining ¼ cup sugar and cinnamon in small bowl. Roll balls of dough in cinnamon-sugar mixture. Place 2 inches apart on ungreased baking sheets.

4. Bake at 400°F for 7 to 8 minutes. Remove to wire racks to cool completely.

Makes 6 dozen cookies

COFFEE FROSTING

1 tablespoon instant coffee
    granules
1 tablespoon hot water
6 tablespoons butter,
    softened

1 teaspoon vanilla
3 cups sifted powdered sugar
$\frac{1}{4}$ to $\frac{1}{3}$ cup whipping cream

Dissolve coffee granules in water. Beat 6 tablespoons butter in medium bowl until soft. Stir in coffee mixture and 1 teaspoon vanilla. Add powdered sugar; mix until well combined. Gradually add cream until good spreading consistency.

Favorite recipe from Wisconsin Milk Marketing Board

SESAME-ALMOND COOKIES

1 cup FILIPPO BERIO® Brand
    Olive Oil
1 (2-inch) strip lemon peel
4 teaspoons sesame seeds
$\frac{1}{2}$ cup dry white wine
1 teaspoon grated lemon
    peel

1 teaspoon grated orange
    peel
$\frac{1}{3}$ cup sugar
$\frac{1}{2}$ cup sliced almonds
$3\frac{1}{2}$ cups all-purpose flour
1 tablespoon ground
    cinnamon

1. Heat oil, 2-inch strip lemon peel and sesame seeds in large skillet over medium heat until seeds are lightly browned. Remove from heat; cool.

2. Remove lemon peel strip. Pour oil and sesame seeds into large bowl. Add wine, grated lemon and orange peels, sugar and almonds; stir.

3. Combine flour and cinnamon in small bowl. Add to oil mixture gradually, stirring well. Gather dough into ball; knead once or twice until smooth. Set aside to rest for 30 minutes.

4. Preheat oven to 350°F. Divide dough into 18 equal pieces. Roll each into a ball and flatten to about 3 inches across and $\frac{1}{4}$ inch thick. Place on lightly greased baking sheet. Bake 20 minutes or until lightly browned and firm. Cool on wire rack. Store in covered container.

Makes 18 cookies

PEANUT BUTTER PIZZA COOKIES

2 packages DUNCAN HINES®
  Peanut Butter
  Cookie Mix
2 eggs
1 tablespoon water
  Sugar
1 container (16 ounces)
  DUNCAN HINES®
  Chocolate Layer Cake
  Frosting

Cashews
Candy-coated chocolate
  pieces
Gumdrops, halved
Flaked coconut
1 bar (2 ounces) white
  chocolate baking bar
1 tablespoon CRISCO®
  Shortening

1. Preheat oven to 375°F.

2. For cookies, place cookie mixes in large bowl. Break up any lumps. Add eggs, contents of peanut butter packets from Mixes and water. Stir until thoroughly blended. Shape into 18 (2-inch) balls (about 3 level tablespoons each). Place 3½ inches apart on ungreased baking sheets. Flatten with bottom of large glass dipped in sugar to make 3-inch circles. Bake at 375°F for 9 to 11 minutes or until set. Cool 1 minute on baking sheets. Remove to cooling racks. Cool completely.

3. Frost cookies with Chocolate frosting. Decorate with cashews, chocolate pieces, gumdrops and coconut. Melt white chocolate and shortening in small saucepan on low heat, stirring constantly until smooth. Drizzle over cookies. *Makes 18 (3-inch) cookies*

CAP'N'S COOKIES

1 cup firmly packed brown
  sugar
½ cup (1 stick) margarine or
  butter, softened
2 eggs
1 teaspoon vanilla
1½ cups all-purpose flour

1 teaspoon baking powder
½ teaspoon salt (optional)
2 cups CAP'N CRUNCH®
  Cereal, any flavor,
  coarsely crushed
1 cup raisins or semi-sweet
  chocolate pieces

Heat oven to 375°F. Lightly grease cookie sheet. Beat sugar and margarine until fluffy. Blend in eggs and vanilla. Add combined flour, baking powder and salt; mix well. Stir in cereal and raisins. Drop by rounded teaspoonfuls onto prepared cookie sheet. Bake 10 to 12 minutes or until light golden brown. Cool 2 minutes on cookie sheet; remove to wire rack. Cool completely. Store tightly covered. *Makes about 3 dozen cookies*

Peanut Butter Pizza Cookies

Mini Morsel Granola Cookies and Banana Bars (page 63)

MINI MORSEL GRANOLA COOKIES

2½ cups all-purpose flour
  2 teaspoons baking powder
  1 teaspoon baking soda
  1 teaspoon cinnamon
  1 cup (2 sticks) butter,
    softened
1¼ cups firmly packed brown
    sugar

  2 eggs
One 12-ounce package (2 cups)
    NESTLÉ® Toll House®
    semi-sweet chocolate
    mini morsels
  2 cups granola cereal
  1 cup raisins

Preheat oven to 375°F. In small bowl, combine flour, baking powder, baking soda and cinnamon; set aside.

In large mixer bowl, beat butter and brown sugar until creamy. Beat in eggs. Gradually beat in flour mixture. Stir in Nestlé Toll House semi-sweet chocolate mini morsels, granola and raisins. Drop by rounded measuring tablespoonfuls onto ungreased cookie sheets.

Bake 9 to 11 minutes until edges are golden brown. Let stand on cookie sheets 5 minutes. Remove from cookie sheets; cool.

Makes about 4 dozen cookies

NORWEGIAN MOLASSES COOKIES

2¼ cups all-purpose flour
2 teaspoons baking soda
1 cup firmly packed light
 brown sugar
¾ cup FLEISCHMANN'S®
 Margarine, softened
¼ cup EGG BEATERS® 99%
 Real Egg Product

¼ cup BRER RABBIT® Light
 or Dark Molasses
¼ cup granulated sugar
Water
Confectioner's Sugar Glaze
 (recipe follows) (optional)
Colored sprinkles
 (optional)

In small bowl, combine flour and baking soda; set aside.

In medium bowl with electric mixer at medium speed, cream brown sugar and margarine. Add egg product and molasses; beat until smooth. Stir in flour mixture. Cover; chill dough 1 hour.

Shape dough into 48 (1¼-inch) balls; roll in granulated sugar. Place on greased and floured baking sheets, about 2 inches apart. Lightly sprinkle dough with water. Bake at 350°F for 18 to 20 minutes or until flattened. Remove from sheets; cool on wire racks. Decorate with Confectioner's Sugar Glaze and colored sprinkles if desired.   *Makes 4 dozen cookies*

Confectioner's Sugar Glaze: Combine 1 cup confectioner's sugar and 5 to 6 teaspoons skim milk.

GIANT OATMEAL COOKIES

1 cup firmly packed brown
 sugar
¾ cup (1½ sticks) margarine
 or butter, softened
2 eggs
1 teaspoon vanilla
1¼ cups all-purpose flour
½ teaspoon baking soda

½ teaspoon salt (optional)
2½ cups QUAKER® Oats (quick
 or old fashioned,
 uncooked)
One 6-ounce package (1 cup)
 semi-sweet chocolate
 pieces
½ cup chopped nuts

Heat oven to 350°F. Lightly grease 2 large cookie sheets. Beat sugar and margarine until fluffy. Blend in eggs and vanilla. Add combined flour, baking soda, salt and oats; mix well. Stir in chocolate pieces and nuts. Divide dough in half. Press each half into circle about ¾ inch thick on prepared cookie sheets. Bake 17 to 20 minutes or until lightly browned. Cool 5 minutes on cookie sheets; remove to wire racks. Cool completely. Cut into wedges to serve.   *Makes 2 giant cookies*

Variation: Drop dough by rounded tablespoonfuls onto greased cookie sheets. Bake 10 to 12 minutes. Makes about 3 dozen cookies.

OATMEAL SCOTCHIES

1¼ cups all-purpose flour
1 teaspoon baking soda
½ teaspoon salt
½ teaspoon cinnamon
1 cup (2 sticks) butter,
  softened
¾ cup granulated sugar
¾ cup firmly packed brown
  sugar
2 eggs

1 teaspoon vanilla extract *or*
  grated peel of 1 orange
3 cups quick or old
  fashioned oats,
  uncooked
One 12-ounce package (2 cups)
  NESTLÉ® Toll House®
  butterscotch flavored
  morsels

Preheat oven to 375°F. In small bowl, combine flour, baking soda, salt and cinnamon; set aside.

In large mixer bowl, beat butter, granulated sugar, brown sugar, eggs and vanilla extract until creamy. Gradually beat in flour mixture. Stir in oats and Nestlé Toll House butterscotch flavored morsels. Drop by measuring tablespoonfuls onto ungreased cookie sheets. Bake 7 to 8 minutes for chewier cookies (9 to 10 minutes for crisper cookies). Remove from cookie sheets; cool completely.   *Makes about 4 dozen cookies*

PEANUT BUTTER COOKIES

⅔ cup firmly packed light
  brown sugar
½ cup chunky or smooth
  peanut butter
⅓ cup BLUE BONNET®
  Margarine, softened
1 egg

½ cup Regular, Instant or
  Quick CREAM OF
  WHEAT® Cereal
1 teaspoon vanilla extract
1¼ cups all-purpose flour
½ teaspoon baking soda

In medium bowl with electric mixer at medium speed, beat brown sugar, peanut butter, margarine and egg until fluffy; blend in cereal and vanilla. Stir in flour and baking soda to make a stiff dough.

Shape dough into 1-inch balls. Place 2 inches apart on greased baking sheets. Flatten balls with bottom of floured glass; press with fork tines to make criss-cross pattern. Bake at 350°F for 8 to 9 minutes or until lightly browned. Remove from sheets; cool on wire racks.

Makes 4 dozen cookies

Oatmeal Scotchies

Lunch Box Lollipops

FAMOUS OATMEAL COOKIES

¾ cup vegetable shortening
1 cup firmly packed brown
    sugar
½ cup granulated sugar
1 egg
¼ cup water
1 teaspoon vanilla

3 cups QUAKER® Oats (quick
    or old fashioned,
    uncooked)
1 cup all-purpose flour
1 teaspoon salt (optional)
½ teaspoon baking soda

Heat oven to 350°F. Beat shortening, sugars, egg, water and vanilla until
creamy. Add combined oats, flour, salt and baking soda; mix well. Drop by
rounded teaspoonfuls onto ungreased cookie sheet. Bake 12 to 15 minutes
or until light golden brown. Remove to cooling rack; cool completely.
Store tightly covered.   *Makes about 5 dozen cookies*

My Own Special Cookies: Add 1 cup of any or a combination of the
following ingredients to basic cookie dough: raisins, chopped nuts,
chocolate chips or coconut. Makes about 5 dozen cookies.

LUNCH BOX LOLLIPOPS

2 extra-ripe, medium DOLE®
   Bananas
¾ cup brown sugar, packed
¾ cup margarine, softened
1 egg
1¾ cups quick-cooking oats
1½ cups all-purpose flour
1 teaspoon ground
   cinnamon

½ teaspoon ground nutmeg
½ teaspoon baking soda
½ teaspoon salt
1½ cups DOLE® Raisins
1 cup DOLE® Chopped
   Almonds
4 dozen wooden popsicle
   sticks (optional)

• Place bananas in blender. Process until puréed; use 1 cup for recipe.

• Beat brown sugar and margarine in large bowl until light and fluffy. Beat in egg, then 1 cup banana.

• Combine oats, flour, cinnamon, nutmeg, baking soda and salt in small bowl; stir into banana mixture just until blended. Stir in raisins and almonds.

• Drop by 2 heaping tablespoonfuls, 2 inches apart, onto lightly greased cookie sheets. Push popsicle stick into center of each, if desired. Flatten tops of cookies with back of spoon.

• Bake in 350°F oven 15 to 18 minutes until lightly browned. Cool on wire racks. *Makes 3½ to 4 dozen cookies*

SOFT RAISIN COOKIES

1 cup butter, softened
¾ cup packed brown sugar
½ cup granulated sugar
2 eggs
1½ teaspoons vanilla
3 cups all-purpose flour
½ cup wheat germ

2 teaspoons baking powder
¾ teaspoon baking soda
½ teaspoon salt
½ teaspoon nutmeg
½ cup milk
1 cup raisins

Beat butter, sugars, eggs and vanilla in large mixer bowl. Combine flour, wheat germ, baking powder, baking soda, salt and nutmeg in medium bowl. Add to butter mixture alternately with milk, mixing well after each addition. Stir in raisins. Drop dough by teaspoonfuls, 2 inches apart, onto ungreased cookie sheets. Bake in 350°F oven 10 to 12 minutes or until light brown. Immediately remove to wire racks to cool.

Makes about 7 dozen cookies

Favorite recipe from Wisconsin Milk Marketing Board

Outrageous Brownies & Bars

Rich brownies and delicious bar cookies are quick to make and will satisfy the cookie monster in your house.

ONE BOWL BROWNIES

4 squares BAKER'S®
   Unsweetened Chocolate
¾ cup (1½ sticks) margarine
   or butter
2 cups sugar

3 eggs
1 teaspoon vanilla
1 cup all-purpose flour
1 cup chopped nuts
   (optional)

Heat oven to 350°F. Microwave chocolate and margarine in large microwavable bowl on HIGH 2 minutes or until margarine is melted. Stir until chocolate is completely melted. Stir sugar into melted chocolate mixture. Mix in eggs and vanilla until well blended. Stir in flour and nuts. Spread in greased 13×9-inch pan.

Bake 30 to 35 minutes or until toothpick inserted into center comes out with fudgy crumbs. *Do not overbake.* Cool in pan; cut into bars.

Makes about 24 brownies

Prep time: 10 minutes
Baking time: 30 to 35 minutes

Tips:
• For cakelike brownies, stir in ½ cup milk with eggs and vanilla. Increase flour to 1½ cups.

• When using a glass baking dish, reduce oven temperature to 325°F.

Continued on page 60

Top to bottom: Peanut Butter Swirl Brownies (page 60); Rocky Road Brownies (page 60)

Rocky Road Brownies: Prepare One Bowl Brownies as directed. Bake at 350°F for 30 minutes. Sprinkle 2 cups KRAFT® Miniature Marshmallows, 1 cup BAKER'S® Semi-Sweet Real Chocolate Chips and 1 cup chopped nuts over brownies immediately. Continue baking 3 to 5 minutes or until topping begins to melt together. Cool in pan; cut into bars. Makes about 24 brownies.

Prep time: 15 minutes
Baking time: 35 minutes

Peanut Butter Swirl Brownies: Prepare One Bowl Brownie batter as directed, reserving 1 tablespoon margarine and 2 tablespoons sugar. Spread batter in greased 13×9-inch pan. Add reserved ingredients to ⅔ cup peanut butter; mix well. Place spoonfuls of peanut butter mixture over brownie batter. Swirl with knife to marbleize. Bake at 350°F for 30 to 35 minutes or until toothpick inserted into center comes out with fudgy crumbs. Cool in pan; cut into bars. Makes about 24 brownies.

Prep time: 15 minutes
Baking time: 30 to 35 minutes

PECAN TURTLE BARS

1½ cups all-purpose flour
1½ cups packed brown sugar, divided
½ cup butter, softened

1 cup pecan halves
⅔ cup butter
1 cup milk chocolate pieces

Combine flour, 1 cup brown sugar and softened butter in large mixer bowl. Beat at medium speed of electric mixer 2 to 3 minutes or until mixture resembles fine crumbs. Pat mixture evenly onto bottom of ungreased 13×9-inch baking pan. Sprinkle pecans evenly over crumb mixture.

Combine ⅔ cup butter and remaining ½ cup brown sugar in small saucepan. Cook and stir over medium heat until entire surface is bubbly. Cook and stir ½ to 1 minute more. Pour into pan, spreading evenly over crust. Bake in 350°F oven 18 to 20 minutes or until entire surface is bubbly. Remove from oven; immediately sprinkle with chocolate pieces. Let stand 2 to 3 minutes to allow chocolate to melt; use knife to swirl chocolate slightly. Cool completely in pan on wire rack. Use sharp knife to cut into 48 bars. *Makes 48 bars*

Favorite recipe from Wisconsin Milk Marketing Board

BLACK RUSSIAN BROWNIES

4 squares (1 ounce *each*) unsweetened chocolate	2 tablespoons vodka
1 cup butter	1⅓ cups all-purpose flour
¾ teaspoon black pepper	½ teaspoon salt
4 eggs, lightly beaten	¼ teaspoon baking powder
1½ cups sugar	1 cup chopped walnuts or toasted sliced almonds
1½ teaspoons vanilla	Powdered sugar (optional)
⅓ cup KAHLÚA®	

Line bottom of 13×9-inch baking pan with waxed paper. Melt chocolate and butter with pepper in small saucepan over low heat. Remove from heat.

Combine eggs, sugar and vanilla in large bowl; beat well. Stir in cooled chocolate mixture, Kahlúa and vodka. Combine flour, salt and baking powder; add to chocolate mixture and stir until blended. Add walnuts. Spread in prepared pan.

Bake in 350°F oven just until toothpick inserted into center comes out clean, about 25 minutes. *Do not overbake.* Cool in pan on wire rack. Cut into bars. Sprinkle with powdered sugar, if desired.

Makes about 30 brownies

BAKED S'MORES

1 package DUNCAN HINES® Golden Sugar Cookie Mix	3 bars (1.55 ounces each) milk chocolate
1 egg	1 jar (7 ounces) marshmallow creme
1 tablespoon water	

1. Preheat oven to 350°F. Grease 8-inch square pan.

2. Combine cookie mix, contents of buttery flavor packet from Mix, egg and water in large bowl. Stir until thoroughly blended. Divide cookie dough in half. Press half the dough evenly into bottom of pan.

3. Cut each milk chocolate bar into 12 sections by following division marks on bars. Arrange chocolate sections into 4 rows, with 9 sections in each row.

4. Place spoonfuls of marshmallow creme on top of chocolate. Spread to cover chocolate and cookie dough. Drop remaining cookie dough by teaspoonfuls on top of marshmallow creme. Spread slightly with back of spoon. Bake at 350°F for 25 to 30 minutes or until light golden brown. Cool completely. Cut into squares.

Makes 9 squares

FRUIT AND CHOCOLATE DREAM SQUARES

TOPPING
- ²/₃ cup all-purpose flour
- ½ cup pecans, chopped
- ⅓ cup firmly packed brown sugar
- 6 tablespoons (¾ stick) butter, softened

CRUST
- 1¼ cups all-purpose flour
- ½ cup granulated sugar
- ½ cup (1 stick) butter
- ½ cup strawberry or raspberry jam
- One 11½-ounce package (2 cups) NESTLÉ® Toll House® milk chocolate morsels

Topping: In small bowl, combine ²/₃ cup flour, pecans and brown sugar. With pastry blender or 2 knives, cut in 6 tablespoons butter until mixture resembles coarse crumbs; set aside.

Crust: Preheat oven to 375°F. Grease 9-inch square baking pan. In small bowl, combine 1¼ cups flour and granulated sugar. With pastry blender or 2 knives, cut in ½ cup butter until mixture resembles fine crumbs. Press into prepared pan.

Bake 20 to 25 minutes until set but not brown. Spread with jam. Top with Nestlé Toll House milk chocolate morsels and Topping.

Bake 15 to 20 minutes longer until top is lightly browned. Cool completely; cut into 2¼-inch squares. *Makes 16 squares*

PEANUT BUTTER-RAISIN BARS

- ¼ cup firmly packed light brown sugar
- ¼ cup corn syrup
- ¼ cup chunky peanut butter
- 2 cups SPOON SIZE® Shredded Wheat, coarsely crushed
- ¾ cup seedless raisins

In large saucepan over medium heat, stir together brown sugar and corn syrup until sugar dissolves and mixture is warm. Remove from heat; blend in peanut butter. Stir in cereal and raisins until well coated. Press into lightly greased 8×8-inch baking pan. Cool until firm. Cut into 24 bars. Store in airtight container. *Makes 24 bars*

Fruit and Chocolate Dream Squares

BANANA BARS

1½ cups all-purpose flour
½ cup whole wheat flour
2 teaspoons baking powder
½ teaspoon salt
¾ cup (1½ sticks) butter, softened
⅔ cup granulated sugar
⅔ cup firmly packed light brown sugar

1 teaspoon vanilla extract
2 medium bananas, mashed
1 egg
One 12-ounce package (2 cups) NESTLÉ® Toll House® semi-sweet chocolate mini morsels
Confectioners' sugar

Preheat oven to 350°F. In small bowl, combine flours, baking powder and salt; set aside.

In large mixer bowl, beat butter, granulated sugar, brown sugar and vanilla extract until creamy. Beat in bananas and egg. Gradually beat in flour mixture. Stir in Nestlé Toll House semi-sweet chocolate mini morsels. Spread into greased 15½ × 10½-inch baking pan.

Bake 25 to 30 minutes. Cool completely. Sprinkle with confectioners' sugar. Cut into 2 × 1-inch bars.   *Makes about 6½ dozen bars*

Variation: Omit whole wheat flour. Increase all-purpose flour to 2 cups.

PINEAPPLE PECAN BARS

CRUST

2 cups all-purpose flour

⅔ cup powdered sugar

1 cup margarine

PINEAPPLE TOPPING

1 can (20 ounces) DOLE®
    Crushed Pineapple in
    Syrup or Juice, drained

4 eggs

¾ cup brown sugar, packed

⅓ cup all-purpose flour

2 cups coarsely chopped
    pecans

For crust, combine 2 cups flour and powdered sugar. Cut in margarine until mixture is crumbly. Press into bottom of 13×9-inch baking pan. Bake in 350°F oven 15 minutes. Remove from oven.

For topping, combine drained pineapple, eggs, brown sugar and ⅓ cup flour. Stir in pecans. Pour over partially baked crust. Bake in 350°F oven 30 to 35 minutes or until set. Cool completely. Cut into bars.

Makes 32 bars

MALLOW-GRAHAM BARS

2 tablespoons BLUE
    BONNET® Margarine

3 cups marshmallows

1 stay fresh package HONEY
    MAID® Honey Grahams,
    coarsely chopped

½ cup seedless raisins

½ cup chopped dry roasted
    peanuts

In large saucepan over low heat, melt margarine. Add marshmallows; stir until melted. Remove from heat; stir in graham crackers, raisins and peanuts. Spread mixture into greased 9×9-inch baking pan. Cool 1 hour or until firm. Cut into 18 bars. Store in airtight container.

Makes 18 bars

Pineapple Pecan Bars

CHOCOLATE PECAN PIE BARS

CRUST
1½ cups all-purpose flour
½ cup (1 stick) butter,
softened

¼ cup firmly packed brown
sugar

FILLING
3 eggs
¾ cup dark or light corn
syrup
¾ cup granulated sugar
2 tablespoons (¼ stick)
butter, melted
1 teaspoon vanilla extract

1½ cups coarsely chopped
pecans
One 12-ounce package (2 cups)
NESTLÉ® Toll House®
semi-sweet chocolate
morsels

Crust: Preheat oven to 350°F. In small mixer bowl, beat flour, ½ cup butter and brown sugar until crumbly. Press into greased 13×9-inch baking pan. Bake 12 to 15 minutes until lightly browned.

Filling: In medium bowl with wire whisk, beat eggs, corn syrup, granulated sugar, melted butter and vanilla extract. Stir in pecans and Nestlé Toll House semi-sweet chocolate morsels. Pour evenly over baked crust.

Bake 25 to 30 minutes until set. Cool; cut into 2×1½-inch bars.

Makes about 3 dozen bars

FUDGY CHEESECAKE SWIRL BROWNIES

CREAM CHEESE BATTER
One 8-ounce package cream
cheese, softened
½ cup sugar

1 egg
1 teaspoon vanilla extract

CHOCOLATE BATTER
¾ cup (1½ sticks) butter
2 foil-wrapped bars
(4 ounces) NESTLÉ®
unsweetened chocolate
baking bars

1¾ cups sugar
3 eggs, well beaten
1¾ cups all-purpose flour

Continued

Fudgy Cheesecake Swirl Brownies

Cream Cheese Batter: Preheat oven to 350°F. In small mixer bowl, beat cream cheese and ½ cup sugar until smooth. Beat in 1 egg and vanilla extract; set aside.

Chocolate Batter: In heavy-gauge, medium saucepan over low heat, melt butter and Nestlé unsweetened chocolate baking bars, stirring until smooth. Stir in 1¾ cups sugar. Blend in 3 eggs. Stir in flour.

Spread Chocolate Batter into greased 13×9-inch baking pan. Spoon Cream Cheese Batter over top. Swirl metal spatula through batters to marbleize.

Bake 30 to 35 minutes until edges begin to pull away from sides of pan. Cool completely; cut into 2-inch bars.

Makes about 2 dozen brownies

Chocolate Apple Crisp

CHOCOLATE APPLE CRISP

1½ cups all-purpose flour
1 cup firmly packed brown sugar
½ teaspoon baking soda
¼ teaspoon salt
¾ cup (1½ sticks) butter
1½ cups quick oats, uncooked

One 12-ounce package (2 cups) NESTLE® Toll House® semi-sweet chocolate mini morsels, divided
3 apples, unpeeled if desired, chopped
1 cup pecans or walnuts, chopped

Preheat oven to 375°F. In large bowl, combine flour, brown sugar, baking soda and salt. With pastry blender or 2 knives, cut in butter until mixture resembles fine crumbs. Stir in oats; press half of oat mixture into greased 13×9-inch baking pan.

To remaining oat mixture, add Nestlé Toll House semi-sweet chocolate mini morsels, apples and pecans; stir to combine. Sprinkle over base.

Bake 35 to 40 minutes until lightly browned. Cool slightly; cut into squares.   *Makes about 15 servings*

MOCHA BROWNIES

1¼ cups all-purpose flour
1 teaspoon baking powder
½ teaspoon salt
4 (1-ounce) squares
  semisweet chocolate
¾ cup BLUE BONNET®
  Margarine
1 tablespoon instant coffee
  granules

1 cup granulated sugar
4 eggs
1 teaspoon vanilla extract
1¼ cups PLANTERS® Walnuts,
  chopped and divided
Creamy Coffee Frosting
  (recipe follows)

In small bowl, combine flour, baking powder and salt; set aside.

In large saucepan over low heat, stir together chocolate, margarine and 1 tablespoon coffee granules until blended. Remove from heat; stir in granulated sugar. Add eggs, 1 at a time, beating well after each addition. Stir in flour mixture and vanilla until blended. Stir in 1 cup walnuts. Spread in greased 13 × 9-inch baking pan.

Bake at 350°F for 25 to 30 minutes. Cool in pan on wire rack. Spread with Creamy Coffee Frosting; sprinkle with remaining ¼ cup walnuts. Cut into 2 × 1½-inch bars.   *Makes about 32 bars*

Creamy Coffee Frosting: Dissolve 1 teaspoon instant coffee granules in ¼ cup milk. In small bowl with electric mixer at high speed, beat 4 ounces cream cheese and milk mixture until creamy. Gradually beat in 1 (16-ounce) package confectioner's sugar until well blended and good spreading consistency.

FROSTED TOFFEE BARS

2 cups QUAKER® Oats (quick
  or old fashioned,
  uncooked)
½ cup firmly packed brown
  sugar

½ cup (1 stick) margarine or
  butter, melted
½ cup semi-sweet chocolate
  pieces
¼ cup chopped peanuts

Heat oven to 350°F. Lightly grease 9-inch square baking pan. In large bowl, combine oats, brown sugar and margarine; mix well. Spread into prepared pan. Bake 13 minutes or until light golden brown; cool on wire rack.

In small saucepan over low heat, melt chocolate pieces. Spread over baked oat mixture; sprinkle with peanuts. Chill 4 hours or until chocolate is set. Cut into 2 × 1½-inch bars. Store tightly covered in refrigerator.
                              Makes about 28 bars

RICH 'N' CREAMY BROWNIE BARS

BROWNIES

1 package DUNCAN HINES®
   Chocolate Lovers' Double
   Fudge Brownie Mix
2 eggs

⅓ cup water
¼ cup CRISCO® Oil or
   CRISCO® PURITAN® Oil
½ cup chopped pecans

TOPPING

1 package (8 ounces) cream
   cheese, softened
2 eggs

1 pound (3½ cups)
   confectioners sugar
1 teaspoon vanilla extract

1. Preheat oven to 350°F. Grease bottom of 13×9-inch pan.

2. **For brownies,** combine brownie mix, contents of fudge packet from Mix, 2 eggs, water and oil in large bowl. Stir with spoon until well blended, about 50 strokes. Stir in pecans. Spread evenly in pan.

3. **For topping,** beat cream cheese in large bowl at medium speed with electric mixer until smooth. Beat in 2 eggs, confectioners sugar and vanilla extract until smooth. Spread evenly over brownie mixture. Bake at 350°F for 45 to 50 minutes or until edges and top are golden brown and shiny. Cool completely. Refrigerate until well chilled. Cut into bars.

Makes 48 bars

SPICED MINCEMEAT SQUARES

½ cup all-purpose flour
½ teaspoon ground
   cinnamon
¼ teaspoon ground nutmeg
¼ teaspoon baking soda
⅓ cup BLUE BONNET®
   Margarine, softened

½ cup firmly packed light
   brown sugar
1 egg
1 cup prepared mincemeat
1 cup NABISCO® 100% Bran
   Confectioner's Sugar Glaze
   (page 53)

In small bowl, combine flour, cinnamon, nutmeg and baking soda; set aside.

In medium bowl with electric mixer at medium speed, beat margarine and brown sugar until creamy. Beat in egg. Add flour mixture, mincemeat and bran. Spread into greased 9×9-inch baking pan. Bake at 400°F for 20 to 25 minutes or until knife inserted into center comes out clean. Cool on wire rack. Drizzle with Confectioner's Sugar Glaze. Cut into 2¼-inch squares. Store in airtight container.

Makes 16 squares

Rich 'n' Creamy Brownie Bars

YUMMY PEANUT BUTTER BARS

BARS
1 package DUNCAN HINES®
   Peanut Butter
   Cookie Mix

1 egg
1 tablespoon water
⅓ cup chopped peanuts

WHITE GLAZE
½ cup confectioners sugar

1 to 2 teaspoons water

CHOCOLATE GLAZE
¼ cup semi-sweet chocolate
   chips

2 teaspoons CRISCO®
   Shortening

1. Preheat oven to 350°F.

2. **For bars,** combine cookie mix, contents of peanut butter packet from Mix, egg and 1 tablespoon water in large bowl. Stir until thoroughly blended. Stir in peanuts. Spread in ungreased 8-inch square pan. Bake at 350°F for 23 to 25 minutes or until edges are light golden brown. Cool completely.

3. **For white glaze,** place confectioners sugar in small bowl. Add water, 1 teaspoon at a time, stirring until smooth and desired consistency. Drizzle over cooled bars.

4. **For chocolate glaze,** place chocolate chips and shortening in small resealable plastic bag; seal. Place bag in bowl of hot water for several minutes. Dry with paper towel. Knead until blended and chocolate is smooth. Snip pinpoint hole in corner of bag. Drizzle chocolate glaze over white glaze. Allow glazes to set before cutting into bars.

Makes 18 bars

Tip: For a special presentation, cut cookies into diamond or triangle shapes instead of bars.

RASPBERRY MERINGUE BARS

1 cup butter or margarine,
   softened
½ cup firmly packed brown
   sugar

1 egg
2 cups all-purpose flour
1 can SOLO® *or* 1 jar BAKER®
   Raspberry Filling

MERINGUE TOPPING
3 egg whites
¾ cup granulated sugar

½ cup shredded coconut
½ cup slivered almonds

Continued

Preheat oven to 325°F. Grease 13×9-inch baking pan. Beat butter and brown sugar in medium bowl with electric mixer at medium speed until light and fluffy. Add 1 egg; beat until blended. Stir in flour until well combined. Pat dough evenly in prepared pan. Bake 20 minutes. Remove from oven; spread raspberry filling over crust. (Do not turn oven off.)

For meringue topping, beat egg whites in medium bowl with electric mixer at high speed until soft peaks form. Add granulated sugar gradually; beat until stiff and glossy. Fold coconut and almonds into beaten egg white mixture. Spread over raspberry filling. Return to oven. Bake 20 minutes or until meringue topping is lightly browned. Cool completely in pan on wire rack. Cut into 48 bars.   *Makes 48 bars*

KAHLÚA® MUDSLIDE BROWNIES

2 cups all-purpose flour
½ teaspoon baking powder
½ teaspoon salt
⅔ cup butter
4 squares (1 ounce *each*) unsweetened chocolate, chopped
3 eggs
1½ cups granulated sugar
4 tablespoons KAHLÚA®

2 tablespoons Irish cream liqueur
1 tablespoon vodka
¾ cup coarsely chopped walnuts (optional)
Kahlúa® Glaze (recipe follows)
Whole coffee beans (optional)

Combine flour, baking powder and salt in small bowl. Melt butter and chocolate in small saucepan over low heat; set aside. Beat eggs and granulated sugar in large bowl until light. Beat in flour mixture, chocolate mixture, 4 tablespoons Kahlúa, Irish cream and vodka. Fold in walnuts. Pour into greased 13×9-inch baking pan.

Bake in 350°F oven just until toothpick inserted into center comes out clean, about 25 minutes. *Do not overbake.* Cool in pan on wire rack. Spread with Kahlúa Glaze. Decorate with whole coffee beans, if desired. Cut into squares.   *Makes 24 brownies*

KAHLÚA® GLAZE

1¼ cups powdered sugar   3 tablespoons KAHLÚA®

Beat together powdered sugar and 3 tablespoons Kahlúa in small bowl until smooth.

Banana Gingerbread Bars

BANANA GINGERBREAD BARS

1 extra-ripe, medium DOLE®
  Banana, peeled
1 package (14.5 ounces)
  gingerbread cake mix
½ cup lukewarm water
1 egg
1 small DOLE® Banana,
  peeled and chopped
  (½ cup)

½ cup DOLE® Raisins
½ cup DOLE® Slivered
  Almonds
1½ cups powdered sugar
  Juice from 1 DOLE® Lemon

Continued

- Place medium banana in blender. Process until puréed; use ½ cup for recipe.

- Combine gingerbread mix, water, ½ cup puréed banana and egg in large bowl. Beat well.

- Stir in chopped banana, raisins and almonds.

- Spread batter in greased 13×9-inch baking pan. Bake in 350°F oven 20 to 25 minutes until toothpick inserted in center comes out clean.

- Mix powdered sugar and 3 tablespoons lemon juice in medium bowl to make thin glaze. Spread over warm gingerbread. Cool. Cut into bars. Sprinkle with additional powdered sugar if desired. *Makes 32 bars*

OATMEAL EXTRAVAGANZAS

1 cup all-purpose flour
1½ teaspoons baking powder
½ teaspoon salt
1 cup firmly packed brown
   sugar
¾ cup (1½ sticks) butter,
   softened
1 teaspoon vanilla extract

1 egg
2 tablespoons water
2 cups quick oats, uncooked
One 12-ounce package (2 cups)
   NESTLÉ® Toll House®
   semi-sweet chocolate
   morsels

Preheat oven to 375°F. In small bowl, combine flour, baking powder and salt; set aside.

In large mixer bowl, beat brown sugar, butter and vanilla extract until creamy. Beat in egg. Gradually blend in flour mixture, then water. Stir in oats and Nestlé Toll House semi-sweet chocolate morsels. Spread in greased 9-inch square pan.

Bake 30 to 35 minutes. Cool; cut into 1½-inch squares.
Makes 3 dozen squares

Fanciful Cookies

Beautiful to look at and great-tasting, these cookies take a little extra time to prepare— but they're worth it!

CHOCOLATE-GILDED DANISH SUGAR CONES

½ cup butter or margarine,
   softened
½ cup sugar
½ cup all-purpose flour
 2 egg whites

1 teaspoon vanilla
3 ounces bittersweet
   chocolate *or* ½ cup
   semisweet chocolate
   chips

Preheat oven to 400°F. Generously grease 4 cookie sheets. Beat butter and sugar in large bowl until light and fluffy. Blend in flour. In clean, dry bowl, beat egg whites until frothy. Blend into butter mixture with vanilla.

Using measuring teaspoon, place 4 mounds of dough, 4 inches apart, on each prepared cookie sheet. Spread mounds with back of spoon dipped in water to 3-inch diameter. Bake, 1 sheet at a time, 5 to 6 minutes or until edges are just barely golden. (Do not overbake or cookies become crisp too quickly and are difficult to shape.) Remove from oven and quickly loosen each cookie from cookie sheet with thin spatula. Shape each into a cone; cones become firm as they cool. (If cookies become too firm to shape, return to oven for a few seconds to soften.)

Melt chocolate in small bowl over hot, not boiling, water. Stir until smooth. When all cookies are baked and cooled, dip flared ends into melted chocolate. Let stand until chocolate is set. If desired, serve cones by standing them in a bowl. (Adding about 1 inch of sugar to bottom of bowl may be necessary to hold them upright.) *Makes 16 cookies*

Chocolate-Gilded Danish Sugar Cones

Orange Pecan Gems

SNOW CAPS

3 egg whites
¼ teaspoon cream of tartar
¾ cup sugar
½ teaspoon vanilla extract
1 cup (6 ounces) semi-sweet
  chocolate chips

2 white chocolate baking
  bars (2 ounces each),
  chopped (optional)

Preheat oven to 200°F. Line baking sheets with parchment paper. In large
mixer bowl, combine egg whites and cream of tartar. Beat at highest
speed of electric mixer until mixture is just frothy. Add sugar, 1
tablespoon at a time, beating well after each addition. Beat until stiff
peaks form. Add vanilla; beat 1 minute. Fold in chocolate chips. Drop
mixture by teaspoonfuls, 1 inch apart, onto prepared baking sheets. Bake
2 hours or until meringues are thoroughly dry to touch but not browned,
rotating baking sheets halfway through baking. Turn off heat. Leave in
closed oven 3 to 4 hours or until completely dry. Remove from oven. Cool
completely. Carefully remove from parchment.

Melt white chocolate in top of double boiler over hot, not boiling, water.
Stir constantly until chocolate melts. Dip top of each cookie into melted
chocolate, if desired. Place on waxed paper to dry. Store at room
temperature in tightly covered containers.

Makes about 6 dozen cookies

ORANGE PECAN GEMS

1 package DUNCAN HINES®
   Moist Deluxe Orange
   Supreme Cake Mix
1 container (8 ounces)
   vanilla lowfat yogurt

1 egg
2 tablespoons butter or
   margarine, softened
1 cup finely chopped pecans
1 cup pecan halves

1. Preheat oven to 350°F. Grease baking sheets.

2. Combine cake mix, yogurt, egg, butter and chopped pecans in large bowl. Beat at low speed with electric mixer until blended. Drop by rounded teaspoonfuls 2 inches apart onto greased baking sheets. Press pecan half onto center of each cookie. Bake at 350°F for 11 to 13 minutes or until golden brown. Cool 1 minute on baking sheets. Remove to cooling racks. Cool completely. Store in airtight container.

Makes 4½ to 5 dozen cookies

Tip: Cookies may be stored in an airtight container in freezer for up to 6 months.

HOLIDAY TEATIME TREATS

2 packages (3 ounces each)
   cream cheese, softened
1 cup butter or margarine,
   softened

2 tablespoons sugar
2 cups all-purpose flour

FILLING

½ cup sugar
2 eggs
¼ cup all-purpose flour
1 teaspoon vanilla

1 can SOLO® *or* 1 jar BAKER®
   Apricot or other fruit
   filling
½ cup chopped nuts
   (optional)

Preheat oven to 350°F. Beat cream cheese, butter and 2 tablespoons sugar in medium bowl with electric mixer until fluffy. Stir in 2 cups flour to make soft dough. Divide dough in half. Shape each piece of dough into about 24 (1-inch) balls. Press balls into bottom and up side of ungreased miniature (1¾-inch) muffin cups. Set aside.

To make filling, beat ½ cup sugar, eggs, ¼ cup flour, vanilla and apricot filling in medium bowl with electric mixer until blended. Stir in nuts. Spoon evenly into pastry-lined muffin cups. Bake 25 to 30 minutes or until filling is set and crust is golden. Cool completely in muffin cups on wire racks.

Makes about 4 dozen cookies

CHERRY SURPRISES

1 package DUNCAN HINES®
   Golden Sugar Cookie Mix
36 to 40 candied cherries

½ cup semi-sweet chocolate
   chips
1 teaspoon CRISCO®
   Shortening

1. Preheat oven to 375°F. Grease baking sheets.

2. Prepare cookie mix following package directions. Shape thin layer of dough around each candied cherry. Place 2 inches apart on greased baking sheets. Bake at 375°F for 8 minutes or until set but not browned. Cool 1 minute on baking sheets. Remove to cooling racks. Cool completely.

3. Place chocolate chips and shortening in small resealable plastic bag; seal. Place bag in bowl of hot water for several minutes. Dry with paper towel. Knead until blended and chocolate is smooth. Snip pinpoint hole in corner of bag. Drizzle chocolate over cookies. Allow drizzle to set before storing between layers of waxed paper in airtight container.

Makes 3 to 3½ dozen cookies

Tip: Well-drained maraschino cherries may be substituted for candied cherries.

DATE ORANGE COOKIE PIZZA

½ cup margarine, softened
½ cup brown sugar, packed
 1 cup all-purpose flour
 1 tablespoon orange juice
 1 teaspoon grated DOLE®
   Orange peel

1 package (8 ounces) DOLE®
   Pitted Dates, chopped
½ cup DOLE® Almonds,
   toasted and chopped

• Beat margarine and sugar in large bowl until light and fluffy. Gradually beat in flour until blended. Beat in orange juice and peel, then dates and almonds.

• Form dough into ball. Placed on greased 14-inch pizza pan. Pat to 12-inch cookie.

• Bake in 375°F oven 15 minutes. Cool completely. Cut into 14 to 16 wedges to serve.
Makes 14 to 16 servings

Cherry Surprises

FLORENTINE CUPS

BASE
- 2 cups HONEY ALMOND DELIGHT® brand cereal, crushed to 1 cup
- 1 cup flaked coconut
- ½ cup raisins
- ½ cup all-purpose flour
- 1½ teaspoons grated fresh orange peel
- ½ teaspoon baking powder
- ½ teaspoon ground cinnamon
- ½ cup packed brown sugar
- ⅓ cup butter or margarine
- ¼ cup honey

ICING
- 1 tablespoon butter or margarine, softened
- ½ cup powdered sugar
- 1½ teaspoons orange juice
- Sliced almonds

To prepare base, preheat oven to 350°F. Grease 32 miniature (1¾-inch) muffin cups. In large bowl, combine cereal, coconut, raisins, flour, orange peel, baking powder and cinnamon; mix well and set aside. In small saucepan, combine brown sugar, ⅓ cup butter and honey. Stir over medium heat until butter is melted and brown sugar is dissolved. Pour over cereal mixture; blend well. Place 1 tablespoon mixture in each prepared muffin cup; press firmly. Bake 8 to 10 minutes or until golden brown (cups will be soft). Cool in pan 15 minutes. Loosen edges. Invert onto wire racks. Cool completely.

To prepare icing, in small bowl, beat 1 tablespoon butter, powdered sugar and orange juice until smooth. With pastry tube, pipe a decorative swirl on top of each cup. Garnish with sliced almonds.

Makes 32 cups

MOCHA MINT CRISPS

- 1 cup butter or margarine, softened
- 1 cup granulated sugar
- 1 egg
- ¼ cup light corn syrup
- ¼ teaspoon peppermint extract
- 1 teaspoon powdered instant coffee
- 1 teaspoon hot water
- 2 cups all-purpose flour
- 6 tablespoons HERSHEY'S Cocoa
- 2 teaspoons baking soda
- ¼ teaspoon salt
- Mocha Mint Sugar (page 83)

Continued

Heat oven to 350°F. In large mixer bowl, beat butter and granulated sugar until light and fluffy. Add egg, corn syrup and peppermint extract; mix thoroughly. Dissolve 1 teaspoon instant coffee in water; stir into butter mixture. Stir together flour, cocoa, baking soda and salt; gradually add to butter mixture, blending thoroughly.

Shape dough into 1-inch balls. (Dough may be refrigerated for a short time for easier handling.) Prepare Mocha Mint Sugar. Roll dough balls in sugar mixture. Place on ungreased cookie sheet, about 2 inches apart. Bake 8 to 10 minutes or until no imprint remains when touched lightly. Cool slightly. Remove from cookie sheet to wire rack. Cool completely.

Makes about 4 dozen cookies

Mocha Mint Sugar: In small bowl, stir together ¼ cup powdered sugar, 2 tablespoons crushed hard peppermint candies (about 6 candies) and 1½ teaspoons powdered instant coffee.

OATMEAL CRANBERRY-NUT COOKIES

¾ cup BUTTER FLAVOR CRISCO®
1 cup firmly packed dark brown sugar
¼ cup dark molasses
1 egg
2 tablespoons milk
1½ teaspoons vanilla
1 cup all-purpose flour
1¼ teaspoons cinnamon

½ teaspoon baking soda
½ teaspoon salt
¼ teaspoon allspice
1 cup crushed whole-berry cranberry sauce
½ cup sliced almonds, broken
3 cups quick oats (not instant or old fashioned), uncooked

1. Heat oven to 375°F. Grease baking sheet with Butter Flavor Crisco.

2. Combine Butter Flavor Crisco and brown sugar in large bowl. Beat at medium speed of electric mixer until well blended. Beat in molasses, egg, milk and vanilla.

3. Combine flour, cinnamon, baking soda, salt and allspice. Mix into creamed mixture at low speed until just blended. Stir in cranberry sauce and nuts. Stir in oats with spoon. Drop tablespoonfuls of dough 2 inches apart onto prepared baking sheet.

4. Bake at 375°F for 12 minutes or until set. Cool 2 minutes on baking sheet. Remove to cooling rack. *Makes about 4 dozen cookies*

CANDY SHOP PIZZA

1½ cups all-purpose flour
½ teaspoon baking soda
½ teaspoon salt
10 tablespoons (1¼ sticks) butter, softened
½ cup granulated sugar
½ cup firmly packed brown sugar
1 egg
½ teaspoon vanilla extract
One 12-ounce package (2 cups) NESTLÉ® Toll House® semi-sweet chocolate morsels, divided

½ cup peanut butter
About 1 cup cut-up fruit, such as bananas and strawberries (optional)
About 1 cup chopped candy bars, such as NESTLÉ® CRUNCH® bars, BUTTERFINGER® bars, ALPINE WHITE® bars, GOOBERS® and RAISINETS®

Preheat oven to 375°F. In small bowl, combine flour, baking soda and salt; set aside.

In large mixer bowl, beat butter, granulated sugar and brown sugar until creamy. Beat in egg and vanilla extract. Gradually beat in flour mixture. Stir in 1 cup Nestlé Toll House semi-sweet chocolate morsels. Spread batter in lightly greased 12- to 14-inch pizza pan or 15½ × 10½-inch jelly-roll pan. Bake 20 to 24 minutes or until lightly browned.

Immediately sprinkle remaining 1 cup semi-sweet chocolate morsels over crust; drop peanut butter by spoonfuls onto morsels. Let stand 5 minutes or until soft and shiny. Gently spread chocolate and peanut butter over crust. Top with fruit and candy. Cut into wedges. Serve warm.

Makes about 12 servings

Candy Shop Pizza

PARTY!!

For: THE WHOLE CLASS

Place: SCHOOL GY

Date: T

PINECONE COOKIES

6 tablespoons butter or
   margarine
1/3 cup HERSHEY'S Cocoa
1 cup sugar
2 eggs
1 teaspoon vanilla extract

2 cups all-purpose flour
1/2 teaspoon baking powder
1/2 teaspoon salt
1/4 teaspoon baking soda
Light corn syrup
Sliced almonds

In small saucepan, melt butter over low heat; remove from heat. Add cocoa; blend well. In large mixer bowl, combine sugar, eggs and vanilla; blend in cocoa mixture. Stir together flour, baking powder, salt and baking soda; add to cocoa-sugar mixture, beating until smooth. Refrigerate dough about 1 hour or until firm enough to roll.

Heat oven to 350°F. Roll out small portion of dough between two pieces of waxed paper to 1/8-inch thickness. Cut into pinecone shapes using 2- or 2 1/2-inch oval cookie cutter. Place on lightly greased cookie sheet; lightly brush cookies with corn syrup. Arrange almonds in pinecone fashion; lightly drizzle or brush almonds with corn syrup. Repeat with remaining dough. Bake 7 to 8 minutes or until set. Cool slightly; remove from cookie sheet to wire rack. Cool completely. *Makes about 4 dozen cookies*

ALMOND-RASPBERRY THUMBPRINT COOKIES

1 cup butter or margarine,
   softened
1 cup sugar
1 can SOLO® *or* 1 jar BAKER®
   Almond Filling
2 egg yolks
1 teaspoon almond extract

2 1/2 cups all-purpose flour
1/2 teaspoon baking powder
1/2 teaspoon salt
1 can SOLO® *or* 1 jar BAKER®
   Raspberry or Strawberry
   Filling

Beat butter and sugar in medium bowl with electric mixer until light and fluffy. Add almond filling, egg yolks and almond extract; beat until blended. Stir in flour, baking powder and salt with wooden spoon to make soft dough. Cover; refrigerate at least 3 hours or overnight.

Preheat oven to 350°F. Shape dough into 1-inch balls. Place on ungreased baking sheets, about 1 1/2 inches apart. Press thumb into center of each ball to make indentation. Spoon 1/2 teaspoon raspberry filling into each indentation. Bake 11 to 13 minutes or until edges of cookies are golden brown. Cool on baking sheets 1 minute. Remove from baking sheets; cool completely on wire racks. *Makes about 5 dozen cookies*

SPECIAL CHOCOLATE CHIP SANDWICHES

1 package DUNCAN HINES®
   Chocolate Chip
   Cookie Mix
1 egg
2 teaspoons water

8 ounces chocolate-flavored
   candy coating
¼ cup chopped sliced natural
   almonds

1. Preheat oven to 375°F.

2. Combine cookie mix, contents of buttery flavor packet from Mix, egg and water in large bowl. Stir until thoroughly blended. Drop by rounded teaspoonfuls 2 inches apart onto ungreased baking sheets. Bake at 375°F for 8 to 10 minutes or until light golden brown. Cool 1 minute on baking sheets. Remove to cooling racks. Cool completely.

3. Place chocolate candy coating in small saucepan. Melt on low heat, stirring frequently until smooth.

4. To assemble, spread about ½ teaspoon melted coating on bottom of one cookie; top with second cookie. Press together to make sandwiches. Repeat with remaining cookies. Dip one-third of each sandwich cookie in remaining melted coating and sprinkle with almonds. Place on cooling racks until coating is set. Store between layers of waxed paper in airtight containers. *Makes 18 sandwich cookies*

Special Chocolate Chip Sandwiches

CHECKERBOARD COOKIES

¾ cup plus 1 tablespoon
    butter or margarine,
    softened and divided
2 egg yolks
½ teaspoon vanilla extract

1 package DUNCAN HINES®
    Moist Deluxe Fudge
    Marble Cake Mix
1 egg, lightly beaten

1. Combine ¾ cup butter, egg yolks and vanilla extract in large bowl. Beat at low speed with electric mixer until blended. Set aside cocoa packet from Mix. Gradually add cake mix. Blend well.

2. Divide dough in half. Add cocoa packet and remaining 1 tablespoon butter to half the dough. Knead until well blended and chocolate colored.

3. Roll out yellow dough between two pieces of waxed paper into a 6-inch square. Repeat with chocolate dough. Remove top pieces of waxed paper from yellow and chocolate doughs. Cut each square into twelve ½-inch-wide strips.

4. To assemble, place one strip chocolate dough on plastic wrap. Brush edge with beaten egg. Place one strip yellow dough next to chocolate dough. Brush edge with egg. Repeat with a second chocolate strip, egg and a second yellow strip to make first row. Brush top of row with egg. Prepare second row by stacking strips on first row, alternating yellow over chocolate strips. Brush edge and top of each strip with egg. Repeat for third row to complete one checkerboard bar. Repeat with remaining strips to make second bar. Cover with plastic wrap. Refrigerate 1 hour or until firm enough to slice.

5. Preheat oven to 350°F. Grease baking sheets.

6. Cut checkerboard bars into ¼-inch slices. Place 2 inches apart on greased baking sheets. Bake at 350°F for 7 to 9 minutes or until edges are light golden brown. Cool 1 minute on baking sheets. Remove to cooling racks. Cool completely. Store in airtight containers.

Makes 4 dozen cookies

DELICATE LACE NUT COOKIES

2 (2-ounce) packages
    PLANTERS® Nut Topping
½ cup firmly packed light
    brown sugar
⅓ cup BLUE BONNET®
    Margarine

3 tablespoons all-purpose
    flour
1 tablespoon milk
1 teaspoon vanilla extract

Continued

ACKNOWLEDGMENTS

The publishers would like to thank the companies
and organizations listed below for the use
of their recipes in this publication.

Checkerboard Kitchens, Ralston Purina Company
Dole Food Company, Inc.
Filippo Berio Olive Oil
Hershey Chocolate U.S.A.
Kahlúa Liqueur
Kraft General Foods, Inc.
Nabisco Foods Group
Nestlé Foods Company
The Procter & Gamble Company
The Quaker Oats Company
Sokol and Company
Walnut Marketing Board
Wisconsin Milk Marketing Board

PHOTO CREDITS

The publishers would like to thank the companies
and organizations listed below for the use of
their photographs in this publication.

Dole Food Company, Inc.
Hershey Chocolate U.S.A.
Kraft General Foods, Inc.
Nestlé Foods Company
The Procter & Gamble Company

Index

All-American Chocolate Chip Cookies, 34
Almond Double Chip Cookies, 23
Almond-Raspberry Thumbprint Cookies, 86
Anise Pillows, 16
Auntie Van's Christmas Cookies, 48

Baked S'Mores, 61
Banana Bars, 63
Banana Gingerbread Bars, 74
Bar Cookies
  Baked S'Mores, 61
  Banana Bars, 63
  Banana Gingerbread Bars, 74
  Black Russian Brownies, 61
  Chocolate Apple Crisp, 68
  Chocolate Pecan Pie Bars, 66
  Frosted Toffee Bars, 69
  Fruit and Chocolate Dream Squares, 62
  Fudgy Cheesecake Swirl Brownies, 66
  Kahlúa® Mudslide Brownies, 73
  Mallow-Graham Bars, 65
  Mocha Brownies, 69
  Oatmeal Extravaganzas, 75
  One Bowl Brownies, 58
  Peanut Butter-Raisin Bars, 62
  Peanut Butter Swirl Brownies, 60
  Pecan Turtle Bars, 60
  Pineapple Pecan Bars, 65
  Raspberry Meringue Bars, 72
  Rich 'n' Creamy Brownie Bars, 70
  Rocky Road Brownies, 60
  Spiced Mincemeat Squares, 70
  Toll House Pan Cookies, 24
  Yummy Peanut Butter Bars, 72
Black Russian Brownies, 61

Candy Shop Pizza, 84
Cap'n's Cookies, 50
Checkerboard Cookies, 88
Cherry Pinwheel Slices, 91
Cherry Surprises, 80
Chocolate (*see also*** Chocolate Chips; Cocoa)**
  Baked S'Mores, 61
  Black Russian Brownies, 61
  Checkerboard Cookies, 88
  Cherry Surprises, 80
  Chocolate-Caramel Sugar Cookies, 32
  Chocolate-Gilded Danish Sugar Cones, 76
  Chocolate Lace Cornucopias, 36
  Chocolate Mint Pinwheels, 28

Chocolate Mint Snow-Top Cookies, 31
Chocolate Mint Sugar Cookie Drops, 35
Chocolate Raspberry Linzer Cookies, 30
Chocolate-Raspberry Spritz, 8
Chocolate Sugar Cookies, 32
Christmas Tree Hanging Cookies, 12
Fancy Walnut Brownies, 90
Fudge-Filled Cream Wafers, 92
Fudgy Cheesecake Swirl Brownies, 66
Jam-Filled Chocolate Sugar Cookies, 32
Kahlúa® Mudslide Brownies, 73
Mint Chocolate Chews, 27
Mocha Brownies, 69
Mocha Filling, 34
New Wave Chocolate Spritz Cookies, 30
Nutty Chocolate Stars, 39
One Bowl Brownies, 58
Peanut Butter Pizza Cookies, 50
Peanut Butter Spritz Sandwiches, 40
Peanut Butter Swirl Brownies, 60
Premier White® Sugar Cookies, 12
Rich 'n' Creamy Brownie Bars, 70
Rocky Road Brownies, 60
Snow Caps, 78
Special Chocolate Chip Sandwiches, 87
Yummy Peanut Butter Bars, 72
Chocolate Apple Crisp, 68
Chocolate Chip Lollipops, 27
Chocolate Chips (*see also*** Chocolate; Cocoa)**
  All-American Chocolate Chip Cookies, 34
  Almond Double Chip Cookies, 23
  Banana Bars, 63
  Candy Shop Pizza, 84
  Chocolate Apple Crisp, 68
  Chocolate Chip Lollipops, 27
  Chocolate Chips Thumbprint Cookies, 20
  Chocolate Pecan Pie Bars, 66
  Chocolate-Raspberry Spritz, 8
  Christmas Tree Hanging Cookies, 12
  Chunky Butter Christmas Cookies, 43
  Frosted Toffee Bars, 69
  Fruit and Chocolate Dream Squares, 62
  Giant Oatmeal Cookies, 53
  Merry Spritz Cookies, 8
  Merry Sugar Cookies, 44
  Mini Morsel Granola Cookies, 52
  My Own Special Cookies, 56
  Oatmeal Extravaganzas, 75
  Original Toll House® Chocolate Chip Cookies, 24

Peanut Butter and Chocolate Cookie
  Sandwich Cookies, 38
Peanut Butter Jumbos, 23
Pecan Turtle Bars, 60
Premier White® Sugar Cookies, 12
Refrigerator Toll House Cookies, 24
Rocky Road Brownies, 60
Snow Caps, 78
Special Chocolate Chip Sandwiches, 87
Toll House Pan Cookies, 24
White Chocolate Biggies, 22
Christmas Treasure Nuggets, 17
Christmas Tree Hanging Cookies, 12
Chunky Butter Christmas Cookies, 43
Cocoa
  Chocolate Melting Moments, 34
  Mocha Mint Crisps, 82
  Peanut Butter and Chocolate Cookie
    Sandwich Cookies, 38
  Pinecone Cookies, 86
  White Chocolate Biggies, 22
Coffee Frosting, 49
Creamy Coffee Frosting, 69
Cutout Cookies
  Auntie Van's Christmas Cookies, 48
  Christmas Tree Hanging Cookies, 12
  Gingerbread Cookies, 45
  Glazed Sugar Cookies, 4
  Premier White® Sugar Cookies, 12
  Stained Glass Cookies, 7
  Sugar Cookie Ornaments, 11
  Sugar Cookies, 13

Date Orange Cookie Pizza, 80
Delicate Lace Nut Cookies, 88
Drop Cookies
  All-American Chocolate Chip Cookies, 34
  Almond Double Chip Cookies, 23
  Anise Pillows, 16
  Cap'n's Cookies, 50
  Christmas Treasure Nuggets, 17
  Chunky Butter Christmas Cookies, 43
  Delicate Lace Nut Cookies, 88
  Famous Oatmeal Cookies, 56
  Marvelous Macaroons, 47
  Mini Morsel Granola Cookies, 52
  Mint Chocolate Chews, 27
  My Own Special Cookies, 56
  Oatmeal-Banana Lebkuchen, 16
  Oatmeal Cranberry-Nut Cookies, 83
  Oatmeal Scotchies, 54
  Orange Pecan Gems, 79
  Original Toll House® Chocolate Chip
    Cookies, 24
  Peanut Butter Jumbos, 23
  Pineapple-Oatmeal Cookies, 48
  Pineapple-Raisin Jumbles, 42

Snow Caps, 78
Soft Raisin Cookies, 57
White Chocolate Biggies, 22

Famous Oatmeal Cookies, 56
Fancy Walnut Brownies, 90
Favorite Peanut Butter Cookies, 47
Filling, Mocha, 34
Florentine Cups, 82
Frosted Toffee Bars, 69
Frostings & Glazes
  Coffee Frosting, 49
  Creamy Coffee Frosting, 69
  Kahlúa® Glaze, 73
  Lemon Glaze, 16
Fruit and Chocolate Dream Squares, 62
Fudge-Filled Cream Wafers, 92
Fudge Filling, 92
Fudgy Cheesecake Swirl Brownies, 66

Giant Oatmeal Cookies, 53
Gingerbread Cookies, 45
Glazed Sugar Cookies, 4
Glazes (*see* **Frostings & Glazes**)

Holiday Almond Wreaths, 13
Holiday Teatime Treats, 79

Jam-Filled Chocolate Sugar Cookies, 32

Kahlúa® Glaze, 73
Kahlúa® Mudslide Brownies, 73

Lemon Glaze, 16
Linzer Tarts, 9
Lunch Box Lollipops, 57

Mallow-Graham Bars, 65
Marvelous Macaroons, 47
Merry Spritz Cookies, 8
Merry Sugar Cookies, 44
Mini Morsel Granola Cookies, 52
Miniature Fruitcake Jewels, 89
Mint Chocolate Chews, 27
Mocha Brownies, 69
Mocha Filling, 34
Mocha Mint Crisps, 82
Mocha Mint Sugar, 83
My Own Special Cookies, 56

New Wave Chocolate Spritz Cookies, 30
Norwegian Molasses Cookies, 53
Nutty Chocolate Stars, 39

Oatmeal-Banana Lebkuchen, 16
Oatmeal Extravaganzas, 75
Oatmeal Scotchies, 54

One Bowl Brownies, 58
Orange Pecan Gems, 79
Orange Sugar Cookies, 43
Original Toll House® Chocolate Chip
    Cookies, 24

Peanut Butter
    Candy Shop Pizza, 84
    Favorite Peanut Butter Cookies, 47
    Peanut Butter and Chocolate Cookie
        Sandwich Cookies, 38
    Peanut Butter Cookies, 54
    Peanut Butter Jewels, 45
    Peanut Butter Jumbos, 23
    Peanut Butter Pizza Cookies, 50
    Peanut Butter-Raisin Bars, 62
    Peanut Butter Reindeer, 19
    Peanut Butter Spritz Sandwiches, 40
    Peanut Butter Swirl Brownies, 60
    Yummy Peanut Butter Bars, 72
Pecan Turtle Bars, 60
Pineapple-Oatmeal Cookies, 48
Pineapple Pecan Bars, 65
Pineapple-Raisin Jumbles, 42
Pinecone Cookies, 86
Premier White® Sugar Cookies, 12

Raspberry Meringue Bars, 72
Refrigerator Cookies
    Checkerboard Cookies, 88
    Cherry Pinwheel Slices, 91
    Chocolate Mint Pinwheels, 28
    Refrigerator Toll House Cookies, 24
Rich 'n' Creamy Brownie Bars, 70
Richest Spritz, 15
Rocky Road Brownies, 60

Sandwich Cookies
    Chocolate Raspberry Linzer Cookies,
        30
    Fudge-Filled Cream Wafers, 92
    Linzer Tarts, 9
    Peanut Butter and Chocolate Cookie
        Sandwich Cookies, 38
    Peanut Butter Spritz Sandwiches, 40
    Special Chocolate Chip Sandwiches,
        87
Santa's Thumbprints, 19
Sesame-Almond Cookies, 49
Shaped Cookies
    Almond-Raspberry Thumbprint
        Cookies, 86
    Candy Shop Pizza, 84
    Cherry Surprises, 80
    Chocolate-Caramel Sugar Cookies, 32
    Chocolate Chip Lollipops, 27
    Chocolate Chips Thumbprint Cookies, 20

Chocolate-Gilded Danish Sugar Cones,
    76
Chocolate Lace Cornucopias, 36
Chocolate Melting Moments, 34
Chocolate Mint Snow-Top Cookies, 31
Chocolate Mint Sugar Cookie Drops, 35
Chocolate-Raspberry Spritz, 8
Chocolate Sugar Cookies, 32
Date Orange Cookie Pizza, 80
Fancy Walnut Brownies, 90
Favorite Peanut Butter Cookies, 47
Florentine Cups, 82
Giant Oatmeal Cookies, 53
Holiday Almond Wreaths, 13
Holiday Teatime Treats, 79
Jam-Filled Chocolate Sugar Cookies,
    32
Lunch Box Lollipops, 57
Merry Spritz Cookies, 8
Merry Sugar Cookies, 44
Miniature Fruitcake Jewels, 89
Mocha Mint Crisps, 82
New Wave Chocolate Spritz Cookies,
    30
Norwegian Molasses Cookies, 53
Orange Sugar Cookies, 43
Peanut Butter Cookies, 54
Peanut Butter Jewels, 45
Peanut Butter Pizza Cookies, 50
Peanut Butter Reindeer, 19
Pinecone Cookies, 86
Richest Spritz, 15
Santa's Thumbprints, 19
Sesame-Almond Cookies, 49
Snickerdoodles, 44
Snow-Covered Almond Crescents, 14
Spiced Banana Cookie Wreaths, 14
Sugar Cookie Wreaths, 7
Yuletide Ginger Cookies, 9
Snickerdoodles, 44
Snow Caps, 78
Snow-Covered Almond Crescents, 14
Soft Raisin Cookies, 57
Special Chocolate Chip Sandwiches, 87
Spiced Banana Cookie Wreaths, 14
Spiced Mincemeat Squares, 70
Stained Glass Cookies, 7
Sugar Cookie Ornaments, 11
Sugar Cookies, 13
Sugar Cookie Wreaths, 7

Toll House Pan Cookies, 24

White Chocolate Biggies, 22

Yuletide Ginger Cookies, 9
Yummy Peanut Butter Bars, 72